£3.80

(L01)

£3.80

(L01)

CANAL FRONT
URBAN RENEWAL IN BRUSSELS

CANAL FRONT
URBAN RENEWAL IN BRUSSELS

ATELIER D'ART URBAIN
A R C H I T E C T S

Preface: Michael Crosbie

Text: Charlotte Mikolajczak and Laure Eggericx

Concept and content adviser: Georges Binder

Image and graphic selection adviser: Muriel-Laurence Lambot

images
Publishing

Published in Australia in 2004 by

The Images Publishing Group Pty Ltd

ABN 89 059 734 431

6 Bastow Place, Mulgrave, Victoria, 3170, Australia

Telephone: +61 3 9561 5544 Facsimile: +61 3 9561 4860

Email: books@images.com.au

Website: www.imagespublishinggroup.com

National Library of Australia
Cataloguing-in-Publication entry:

Canal front urban renewal in Brussels.

Includes index.
ISBN 1 876907 38 X.

1. Architecture – Belgium. 2. Brussels (Belgium). I. Atelier d'art urbain.

720.9493

Designed by The Graphic Image Studio Pty Ltd, Mulgrave, Australia
www.tgis.com.au
Film by Mission Productions Limited
Printed by Everbest Printing Co. Ltd. in Hong Kong/China

IMAGES has included on its website a page for special notices in relation to this and our other publications. Please visit this site: www.imagespublishinggroup.com

Contents

Preface

Few great cities are landlocked. As in our own bodies, solid and liquid mingle in nearly all the places where society has built cities. Land and water are the very ingredients of founding an urban center – the elemental ingredients for city-building. The reasons for this are varied. Commerce, of course, is the main progenitor. For many older urban centres, water was the path of commerce, of shipping and receiving, of trade, of exposure to other cultures, which in turn fed and deepened the sophistication of the city dwellers. London, Charleston, Amsterdam, Paris, New Orleans, Venice, New York, Moscow, San Francisco, and Brussels – all of these cities were born out of an urban amniotic fluid that allowed them to commune with the rest of the world, and for the rest of the world to know of them.

Water in the city has other advantages. It is a place of recreation, offering a change in our state of being. To glide upon the water in a pleasure craft is to enjoy an experience quite different to any we can have on land. On water, we view the land differently. We can appreciate buildings and other parts of the built environment from a perspective outside our daily lives. We can see the city anew in a way that our earliest visitors did. And because we can position ourselves on the water in a nearly infinite number of points, our vantage of the city is virtually unique. Moving on the water allows us a constant rediscovery of the places that we thought we knew.

Rivers, oceans, seas and deltas also provide sustenance. Water opens the possibility of trade, but it also offers nutrition in the absence of trade. The ancient profession of fishing brings to urban settlements a culture all its own, created by colourful characters, myth-makers and those fearless enough to slip below and disappear beneath the horizon. Even today, fishing allows an escape from the daily agenda and offers the poorer urban resident a ready way to feed himself. The necessity of approaching the city by water also affords urban dwellers a degree of vigilance in anticipation of attack, which adds to the security of a place of settlement.

Canals take all of the qualities of settlement on water and infuse them through the city. They extend the ribbon of 'water's edge', tracing it through neighbourhoods, linking disparate places in the city. They help us to orient ourselves and change the urban scale. Canals can act as a barrier from one precinct to another, which can magnify the borders of a neighbourhood and restrict its growth, adding to its density and variety. Canals forever hold the possibility of new visitors passing through the city: tourists and traders who might not be seen again.

Humans move differently on water than they do on land. This gives the city another level and scale of activity. People who travel on pavement and pathways can be barely cognisant of those who glide on a canal, and vice versa. Life along the canal is often experienced at a level submerged below the life on the street. Each can have a completely different experience of the same city. The canal can make twists and turns independent of the city grid, offering novel views of architectural landmarks. The presence of a canal in the city makes it possible to design a building that will be experienced and enjoyed at a variety of scales, at a range of speeds and from a plethora of vantage points. The building must respond to both – the canal and the street.

Atelier d'Art Urbain has internalised life on the water and life on the land in its approach to planning and design. The buildings and projects in this book reveal how partners Sefik Birkiye, Dominique Delbrouck, Grégoire de Jerphanion, and Christian Sibilde have successfully married architecture's role on land and its role on water, while at the same time accentuating the building's civic life. In their study of cities on water, they have found commonalities that cross cultures and time periods. They have also discovered the DNA of designing and building in Brussels that gives their architecture a sense of belonging to the city that is immediately recognisable.

Creating such a tight fit between the building, the city and the canal is a much more demanding approach than simply ignoring the context and designing with a 'clean slate'. But the advantages of Atelier d'Art Urbain's approach are worth the struggle. The designers have created modern buildings that are at once products of their age, and also part of the ageless character of Brussels. When you see these projects, you might wonder if they are very old, perhaps restored parts of the city. Some architects would want to avoid such a close association with the context. But not Atelier d'Art Urbain, who sees it as the highest form of praise. In the making of the new, the architects mine the history and physicality of the city, bringing forth from it a new interpretation, not a copy of what has been built before.

The approach of Atelier d'Art Urbain can be transferred to any site in the world. The projects shown in this book outside of the designers' native Belgium reveal a consistent level of close study and comprehension of the unique architectural qualities of the cities in which they work. The designers bring their own appreciation of the richness of cities on the water, and the historical patterns of experience and function to every new context. In this way they extend the fabric of what has come before, adapting it for the way we live today. The result is architecture with a civic presence and an important role to play: to gently remind the city dweller of the civilising forces that urban settlements on the water have always offered.

Michael J. Crosbie

The author is an internationally recognised architectural author, critic and teacher who makes his home on the Connecticut River in Essex, Connecticut, USA.

Sefik Birkiye, founding partner

Christian Sibilde, partner – Dominique Delbrouck, partner – Grégoire de Jerphanion, partner

Interview

The expression 'Canal Front' is made up of two words with very different meanings. Within your own architectural approach, is it the canal or the constructed building fronts that took precedence?

(Sefik Birkiye) Everything started with the canal, which is a powerful element in a city just like a boulevard, but with the benefit of being wider and therefore evoking a different notion of distance. Buildings constructed on the banks of any type of water – canal, river or sea – are seen in perspective, just as they are on a boulevard, but they are also seen front-on, and from a distance. This diversity of viewing angles must always be taken into account in the way these buildings are treated: they can't be simply a façade in a line of façades. And, of course, a canal is not always a quality environment, so the architect has to make sure the building is both visible and spectacular.

(Christian Sibilde) You can even go as far as to say 'monumental'. We shouldn't be frightened of the word. We are a bureau involved in urban architecture. We look at the city from an urban point of view – 'public', 'private', 'perspectives', 'the image of the city' – and we assume our responsibilities. We don't want to create monuments ourselves; it's the location, the site which does that. Now, as has been said, a waterway occupies a very important place in a city. It is an imposing thoroughfare, even if, as in Brussels, it's long been in the doldrums. The water obviously has its part to play, but it is the actual buildings fronting on to it that are visible from everywhere. So two elements are inextricably linked: the monumental nature of the constructed waterfront, and a specific treatment of this arising from its location on the banks of a canal.

Can it be said that with the Canal Front project you were able to do virtually anything you wanted? And at the very least approach it in your own way, with your own subjectivity?

(Sefik Birkiye) Not at all. Even though in Canal Front the canal and the constructions on its banks play a role, it was above all the surrounding district which influenced us and channelled our imagination. A canal has more in common with the idea of industry than with the idea of water; it is more like a railway than a river.

And it also constitutes a frontier, defines a district. That's how we approached the project. We took into account visions specific to this district in preparing this project, and we couldn't – we didn't want to in any case – disregard the proximity of the Tour & Taxis site. But, if we couldn't ignore the historical aspect we equally couldn't confine ourselves to it alone. We had to bring new economic vitality to the district and give it a new image. And so we arrived at this eclectic, broken up construction for the canal bank, using different typologies.

You worked for three different owners: KBC Banking & Insurance for the KBC Bank Headquarters, Betonimmo and Investissements et Promotion for the KBC Bank and Eurobalken for the Green Island building. If you had been working for a single owner, would the whole complex have been completely different?

(Christian Sibilde) Whether for one owner or for three, it was our wish to give a look to the whole complex which was not monolithic.

This formed part of our original conception. In the case of Canal Front, we had to pay extra attention because of the fact that the buildings were all destined for the same use: offices. If other functions had been added (housing, public services, a museum…) then the constructed frontage would have been more eclectic of course.

(Dominique Delbrouck) Fundamentally, this eclecticism would have been expressed in the same way as is found along the thorough-fares of Brussels, where every house is different in its materials, its colours, its details… It is this urban spirit which we wanted to give to this part of the canal, adding the largeness of scale which a public building can sustain.

At the time when these owners were taking an interest in this piece of land, the canal banks in Brussels suffered from a rather negative image. How did you approach, or even attempt to reverse, this image?

(Dominique Delbrouck) Whichever district is in question, it is important that the client benefits from a recognisable image of which he can be proud. And this is even more the case in a district whose image is negative or neutral, and which therefore demands some effort of adhesion.

With the renovation and transformation of the old Nestor Martin foundry into residential accommodation, under the name of Jardin des Fonderies, this phenomenon exceeded all expectations: it is not so much because of the district as because of the architecture that the occupants arrived, and it is thanks to this urban scenario that a genuine spirit of conviviality has grown up amongst them, seen today in common activities such as barbecues, kids' afternoons…

(Christian Sibilde) And this has also been shown to be true with the offices. If the three office buildings on the Canal Front – KBC Bank Headquarters, KBC Bank and Green Island – have this layout, or that atrium, or such and such an interior courtyard, it is above all for the well-being of their occupants, for their comfort, for the view they have to the outside. The rationality of our plans arises essentially from a desire to make those who work in the buildings concerned happy.

Is it possible to speak in terms of a specific 'Atelier d'Art Urbain character'? And if so, what is it?

(Sefik Birkiye) Every architect has his or her own way of going about things. Personally, what interests me is a global approach – and this is as true of architecture as it is of philosophy. I am convinced that the Atelier d'Art Urbain method is exactly this global approach, this synthesising spirit, this positioning relative to the past and to the future, this vision not only of a city, but of life. Its originality comes from the urban struggle, from disputes, from taking the city and its inhabitants into account…

This specific approach dictates a certain method of working. Would you say that this imposes obligations, or even no-go areas?

(Sefik Birkiye) Nothing is forbidden, but there are things that we simply don't do. Our territory is the city. Just the city. You will never find us building an isolated villa out in the country. Within the same spirit, wherever it is possible we go for mixed-use developments. Our knowledge of the past and our vision of the future help us to be certain that man has to live in cities. For reasons as philosophical as they are social, breaking away, dispersing, are the opposites of democracy, of social cohesion. Community life can't take place around a ghetto, whatever happens. The city has to be shared.

The architecture which comes out of Atelier d'Art Urbain is very typical in that it finds its inspiration in the past. Would you say that the past is a springboard to the future and that it allows you to create an architecture of the future?

(Sefik Birkiye) Architecture is always a vision – for us as for any other architect – and a building is a project of the future. Except in the case of pure copying, the architect claims to create a sort of Utopia, very rich in refer-ences or very free-spirited, because he is designing what he thinks will suit both today and tomorrow. Even those most immersed in the past have this claim in mind. The question which most vexes architects is: how to create objects which are more and more specific in nature and how to get away from tradition? The more one doubts oneself, the more one clings on to the tried and tested, to something with a solid foundation. For our part, we use existing buildings to help us exercise our art. For reasons of security. Then we move away from this starting point, we abandon it, and we become the master ourselves, with our own originality. Today we have gone beyond the first phase, we no longer need to start from existing buildings, but from those we have previously created in our bureau.

(Dominique Delbrouck) Our architecture is an interpretation, not a copy, of architectural styles of the past. We take our inspiration from them, then we undertake an abstraction which gives birth to an architectural style of today, a contemporary style. We are a long way from being stuck in the past.

(Grégoire de Jerphanion) By coming back to the source – which is immense – we get closer to the original interpretation. We are better able to synthesise forms and ideas. The past is a language less well known than the present as it is put forward in the media, pre-digested to the limit. But within this past, there are periods we favour: the beginnings of modernism, of industrialisation and, therefore, the styles of Art Deco, of Eclecticism, the urban fabric in general and all its generic expressions.

(Christian Sibilde) This doesn't mean that we shut our eyes to the creations of our neighbours and our contemporaries. We are by no means closed to current images.

With your architecture leaning on the past, does it evolve in line with movements in the past, or more according to the progress of your bureau?

(Grégoire de Jerphanion) Our architecture is evolving, that's undeniable. If the mutations don't seem all that evident, it's sometimes because the changes we would like to make – in terms of materials, tints, forms, building techniques – disturb the owners, the public authorities, the population who, in a certain way, have become 'accustomed' to our approach. To be able to convince them, at least a minimum of maturity is required.

Today, we've reached that stage of maturity. That's why we can now get some new ideas across, change some tastes, alter visual habits. Buildings start to stand out from the crowd when a client, a site or a project allows us more freedom.

(Christian Sibilde) I wouldn't particularly talk in terms of evolution, which would give some buildings an advantage over others. I would rather see it as a widening of the range, a widening of an array of images which support each other in an aesthetic whole, which is now part of our essence.

The final result is changing. Your latest projects, including the Porte de Ninove on the same canal, bear witness to this. But does this mean that working methods have also changed?

(Dominique Delbrouck) It's our experience, our accumulated work, our many buildings, designs, sketches, reflections, which lead us to refine our style and make it even more personal to us. And yet this style, personal as it is, is far from being set in stone. Each of our buildings also comes in for constructive self-criticism. Standing back and taking a critical look is indispensable for us in the sense that it quite simply lets us carry on learning.

(Grégoire de Jerphanion) For the rest, we always go from the complicated, from the detail, towards simplicity, purity. Our work is and remains the search for abstraction, liberation of the superfluous, simplification of proportions and outlines. The Porte de Ninove does not represent a rupture, far from it. Its reference points are perhaps simply less visible, less identifiable than before. In any

case it certainly goes to show that diversity is possible, even along the same canal.

(Sefik Birkiye) This comes from our maturity, but also from the site itself. Where the urban fabric is concerned, we have an attitude tending towards humility – although our signature will be clearly recognisable for posterity.

On other sites, for example along a canal with less obvious reference sites, we are able to be less timid, to go a little further. A city is not an invented concept made up of lots of little bits. That doesn't mean that there is only one vision for a city, however. All the architectural trends which come together in the city have a vision, with underlying political, economic, social and even aesthetic certainties.

What does this mean in terms of the vision of the city, as seen from the perspective of Atelier d'Art Urbain?

(Sefik Birkiye) The city of the past no longer responds to the needs of the present. But it is certainly not our wish to abandon it in favour of some other type of city. We can adapt it, keeping its plus points and modifying them to meet the needs of today's world in terms of density, of reorganisation of the way it is compartmentalised, of its parking facilities, of its mixture of functions… Our objective is to re-work the badly thought out cities of the 19th century, to repair them if you like. And there is one criterion for doing this – to recreate the mixed-function ideals of earlier times, when cities had a market place, a church, a school… The buildings have to be re-created on the bits that remain. They can't break away from this. The architecture which we design is a reflection of ancient architecture, but it is not a copy of it. Our buildings, and the plotting of them, retain the silhouette of old buildings, as do certain of their details. But they are not identical to the old ones. And it is so true to say that our references come just as much from the region in which we are working as from elsewhere in Europe. More important still, and something which we pay great attention to at the moment, is that the buildings we put up must be capable of being transformed and of adapting to different uses from those they were originally designed for. So ground floors, for example, should be able to be transformed into shops if needs be, and offices into housing.

Can it be said of Atelier d'Art Urbain that its first rule is never to disregard the character of the site, whether it is dense, like the Radisson SAS Hotel (virtually an enclave in the city), or open, like the canal banks?

(Christian Sibilde) That sums up all of our history – punctuated by urban struggles, district committees, the reconstruction of cities with a Léon Krier-like degree of mobility… all very well bound into the name we gave to our bureau, the Atelier d'Art Urbain, or Urban Art Workshop. We direct our attention exclusively towards the citizen, the first and only real user of the city. Towards the end of the 1970s, during the post-modernist era when we created Atelier d'Art Urbain, this attention to the citizen was seen as being an innovative trend.

(Grégoire de Jerphanion) Our interest in the quality of the urban environment has always led us to favour the social dimension, the feeling of conviviality, to create spaces and

built areas on a human scale. A building does not exist for its own sake; it forms part of a street, of an environment which we also take into account within its own context. The Canal Front is an excellent example of this: it's not just a monolithic frontage but a scene set on the banks of a canal, lighting it up… It meets its functional needs in a sociable manner, not an egotistical one, and above all it takes account of its occupants.

Does this give you an advantage for difficult projects which may be the subject of competition?

(Sefik Birkiye) An advantage, no. A greater ability to listen, perhaps, not only to the past or to the current context, but also to the local authorities. But, above all, we have a different approach, which allows us to advise the project developer in a different way.

This passion for cities shows itself, above all, in your city, Brussels. Are you tempted by others?

(Sefik Birkiye) Yes, by many. Cities with their own character, their own signature, like New York, London, Edinburgh… And dense cities like Berlin, Paris, Amsterdam, Barcelona. But always cities which are highly sought-after and whose centres have a tradition of mixed functions. In Brussels, the city suffers from being diluted, from a certain monotony of function. Yet our architecture demands multi-functionality: ground floor shops with a greater interface with the outside public areas… In practical terms, as our architecture is built on a knowledge – an understanding – of the areas concerned, we are more easily able to work in neighbouring countries like the

Netherlands, France, Germany, European countries in any case.

Most of the cities you have mentioned are, indeed, European. This confirms your attachment to Europe, to its cities, its history, its past. Yet you have undertaken projects with equal success in other countries and regions, including Turkey, Egypt and the Caribbean, whose culture, art and architecture may appear to be in total contrast to Europe. Using these three examples, did you approach them differently?

(Dominique Delbrouck) With our European culture we can go almost anywhere. We are nevertheless more at ease in cities with a more pronounced European connotation.

In America, for example, we would choose Boston or New York rather than Los Angeles. If we feel ourselves to be in harmony with a city like Cairo, this is because it is half Ottoman, half English. And if we felt a real sense of being in tune with the Caribbean and the Virgin Islands, this is because part of their history, part of their culture, is European.

You have not opened an office in any of the countries in which you have worked, preferring to set up satellites to follow up the work.

(Dominique Delbrouck) We don't want to open offices in other countries, because we would be creating a separate office which does not form part of our objectives. And, in any case, we can't because the control of the project, its conception, the plans, the details… are all done here, and here only, right at the heart of

our team. A team in which, and this is very important, we take pride in perfecting. With all our projects the first objective is to start with a guiding principle, and then to expand, to add on elements arising from our knowledge. Everyone brings in something, always complementary and always in a common spirit. Teamwork is very enriching and allows us to find rapid solutions in all areas: budget and time-scale, as well as architectural, aesthetic and technical characteristics. The complementary spirit which pervades the four of us is repeated throughout the rest of the team, and it is an unparalleled advantage for us.

You say complementary spirit. Others would say team spirit...

(Sefik Birkiye) And I would say philosophy. Because what binds us together is not just an aesthetic method, it is a philosophy which has to spread throughout the whole bureau. At first, we used to speak about it during informal discussions or loosely organised debates in small groups. Then, as the bureau started to grow and the philosophy was more easily recognisable, we were able to structure our way of explaining this philosophy better. The objective was to explain our way of thinking to those who work with us: our own team, from architects to secretaries, as well as sub-contractors and others from the outside who get involved. Currently we are right in between informal discussions and a

more structured approach. We have instigated a series of conferences destined exclusively for our own bureau. By using a series of questions and key words as springboards, we can address some of the major philosophical themes. These range from political thinking to social thinking, and encompass humanism and aestheticism. This cycle will be followed up by something from the aesthetic designers alone.

What is important is that our personnel ask themselves in what way all these reflections influence the way things unfurl, and in what way they can lead them to changing what they produce. The result is, perhaps, what some people would call a 'house spirit'.

What is your architectural ambition for the future?

(Sefik Birkiye) With our 25 years of experience gained in the domain of a typically urban setting principally bound into the history of European cities, our ambition may eventually be to try to create new forms, capable of distinguishing themselves from examples of the past, and of melting into the spirit of the city in which they are created. In a certain way, a sort of contemporary regionalism.

Sefik Birkiye
Dominique Delbrouck
Grégoire de Jerphanion
Christian Sibilde

HISTORICAL ASPECTS

Brussels... one canal, two histories

Brussels is a city that sent its river underground. Nevertheless it has a waterway that crosses the Region from north to south. This canal, wrongly known as the 'Brussels canal', is actually comprised of two canals that come together at the Place Sainctelette: downstream is the Willebroeck canal, and upstream is the Charleroi canal. The construction of this commercial and industrial thoroughfare, which extended over some three centuries and some 17 kilometres, has had a profound effect on its surrounding districts. Along its banks have grown both industries and road networks, housing and sometimes rather prestigious utilitarian buildings. But the most prestigious legacies of this too often misused and ignored thoroughfare, which is often considered a barrier and a divide, are surely the Caserne du Petit Château, the lead tower, the Citroën garage, the Tour & Taxis site, the Godin factory and co-operative, the Buda bridge and on the leisure side the villas belonging to the Nautical Union of Brussels. All these buildings play their part in recounting a turbulent history that stretches back to the 15th century.

The Willebroeck canal – first conceived in the 15th century as a way of mitigating the whims of the Senne, an ill-thought of river even though it was part of the city's origins – was inaugurated in 1561. It linked the capital with the Rupel and was equipped with bridges and locks. Basins and a number of quays and warehouses were constructed inside the city. Brussels thus became a port city. The purchase from the Netherlands of the toll rights on the Escaut (1863), industrial growth and increasing trade led to the filling in of the inner-city basins and the creation of a new port outside the city walls (on the marshy plain towards Laeken and Schaerbeek) and the transformation of the waterway into a maritime canal. Works were completed in 1922. New warehouses and a maritime port grew up, and in the 1930s an advance port was constructed downstream from the bridges at Laeken. From this time on the port and canal formed the spinal cord of an industrial system that brought together supply, transit and exchange and transport services, not only by water but also by road and rail.

The Charleroi canal's objective was to link the Meuse and the Escaut and to transport coal mined in the centre of the country northwards. Nowadays it is a thoroughfare managed (within the limits of the Brussels Central Region) by the Brussels Port Company. It was constructed between 1827 and 1832 in accordance with plans drawn up by the engineer Jean-Baptiste Vifquain, who took his inspiration from the coal-transporting canals of England. The canal was narrow and capable of handling barges with a maximum weight of 70 tonnes – the famous 'bacquets' designed by Vifquain himself – and overcame the crests between the two valleys by means of 55 locks and a one-kilometre tunnel. But it succumbed to the competition posed by the railways after 1870. Successive modernisation works failed to revive the waterway. Its primary objective was removed with the closure of the Hainaut mines, and traffic started to move in the opposite direction. The coal-bearing canal gradually became a transit canal, prolonging the Escaut-Brussels link.

On the Place Sainctelette where it crosses the canal stands a monument erected in honour of the 'developers of the maritime installations'. This monument, the work of artist Auguste De Wever, was put up at the beginning of the 20th century. It was moved in 1956 when the viaduct over the Boulevard Léopold II was built, and then restored and returned to its original site. Two distinctive features of this work are that the man is wearing a fisherman's hat and that he is leaning on an anchor.

Introduction

Canal Front

Every city has its dark corners. Corners which seem to have been left behind in time, places whose inhabitants – if there are any – suffer in silence, places about which visitors can't find a nice word to say. Brussels is no exception, both within its mediaeval perimeter (an ancient pentagon-shaped fortification that is now an inner ring of boulevards) and within its modern suburbs (now 18 separate communes that, together with the commune of Brussels, form the Brussels Capital Region).

At the end of the 1980s, one of these dark corners – one of the most spectacular thanks to the imagined and the imaginary to which it gave rise, and one steeped in industrial history – was the port area located at the northern extreme of the 'Pentagon', alongside the aptly named Avenue du Port. And its inhabitants had not deserted this zone. Several hundred businesses employing almost 10,000 workers coexisted side by side, for better or for worse: industrial concerns, entrepreneurs, transport firms, raw material suppliers, traders, handymen and wheelers and dealers. There was even a bank. But the area looked no less desolate for all that: sinister roads, run-down housing, miserable shops and sad faces. It was a sort of life, but it was dying on its feet.

For a visitor just passing through, this desolation must be astounding, as the city centre is within walking distance and the Rue Neuve – Brussels' most popular, frequented and magnetic shopping street – is so close you can see it. You can also see the Place Rogier; the port zone's opposite neighbour outside the old walls, which spawns hotels like other streets spawn restaurants. Looking in the same direction, you can't fail but to notice the North District, dreamt of in the 1960s as a mini-Manhattan, started in the 1970s, and now after a 15-year hiccup a towering reality just behind the North Station, built in 1956 and enclosed within the larger Centre of Communications. Opposite, you can see the newly renovated Boulevard Léopold II, culminating in the dome of the Koekelberg Basilica before leading onwards to the Brussels—Ghent—Ostend motorway.

The port zone's urban landscape has another attraction: Tour & Taxis, a veritable monument, although abandoned, that is historically symbolic and ripe with potential. It wouldn't take much effort – and certainly not much imagination – to transform this site into a museum, a university, a theatre or a congress centre. Or to pay homage to its past as a seaport, a postal depot and a customs warehouse by transforming it into a vast multi-modal transport hub where both passengers and merchandise could avail themselves of every conceivable type of transport.

And by simply reflecting on the obvious – that a port area means water – any further doubts about the attractiveness of this zone disappear. Not only does water generate added real estate value, but – and you only have to look at New York, London, Paris, Frankfurt, Marseilles, Newcastle or Antwerp – it is also a creative generator.

A Heavy Psychological Weight

Yet, for the people of Brussels the zone's three major characteristics – its proximity to the city centre, its symbolism as a site

TOUR & TAXIS

Waiting for a project worthy of its status

The establishment of the Tour & Taxis site[1] went hand in hand with the development of a port outside the city walls at the end of the 19th century. The site brought together two distinct activities: a railway zone and a customs zone. The buildings, typical of the eclectic industrial architecture crossed with the Flemish Neo-Renaissance style, were built between 1902 and 1907.

The railway zone, designed by the architects C. Bosmans and H. Vandeveld, included the maritime station (or the Merchandise Hangar with its three great metal and glass receptacles), the Postal and Administration building and all the installations, tracks, points and service buildings required for it to function properly.

The customs zone, which was the work of the architect E. Van Humbeek, is comprised of five buildings that incorporated the most modern techniques of the time: the Public Warehouse (or Warehouse B, a veritable fortress of reinforced steel), the Subsidiary (or Warehouse A, which features a metallic self-standing articulated framework and roofing in the form of 'sheds'), the Re-expedition Hall, the Customs House and the repository for dangerous goods.

But this audacious monument, this cathedral of industry, nevertheless saw difficult times despite its unanimously recognised contribution to Brussels' heritage.

The traffic that brought this great trade hub to life gradually dried up. One of the warehouses was decommissioned in 1988 and Belgian Railways (SNCB) left the site in 1994.

However, although activity has ground to a halt on this symbolic 25-hectare site, giving it a somewhat apocalyptic image, Tour & Taxis remains firmly and fondly in the memory of Brussels' inhabitants, more so than at any other time in its 100-year history. It deserves, even demands, a project on a grand scale and has been subjected to the moods of one developer after another and brought to life by the designs of the various public authorities who became involved. Everything, or almost everything, has been envisaged: an entertainment complex, a museum (of railways, of transport, of mobility or immigration since the Second World War), a (national) library, a factory workshop, an international congress centre capable of hosting European summits, an urban distribution centre (of the freight or multi-modal variety) and a vast campus for engineering students within a 'City of Knowledge'.

This last proposal received a sympathetic hearing from the Project T&T company, owners of a large portion (30 hectares) of the site. Within the masterplan established by the American bureau HOK (Hellmuth, Obata & Kassabaum), a part of the site is set aside for precisely this purpose. The remainder is designated for housing, a hotel, offices, a public area with conference rooms, a library, shops and a theatre complex, all traversed by pedestrian walkways.

This ambitious project, whose principal challenge is to develop a new district in harmony with the existing urban fabric, will commence in 2007. The site will not be totally abandoned in the meantime, however. Project T&T is already completing the renovation of the two historical buildings from the ex-customs zone, the Public Warehouse and the Subsidiary (by architectural bureau Archi 2000), which will house offices, non-polluting goods production activities, an exhibition hall, shops and restaurants.

The most spectacular buildings of the Tour & Taxis site are the work of architect Van Humbeek, and were constructed in 1904 and 1907: the 'Hôtel des Douanes' or Customs Hall (on the right in the photo), and the 'Entrepôt Royal et les Magasins' or Royal Depot and Stores (on the left). They display the exceptional know-how of the engineers of the time through the use of metal and the way the light is treated.

1   At the end of the 19th century a large part of the site belonged to the noble von Thurn und Tassis family. Of German origin, this family settled in Brussels and founded the first official European postal service, between Brussels and Vienna, in 1490. The name of the site evolved into 'Tour & Taxis' in French or 'Turn & Taxis' in Flemish.

awaiting renaissance, and its life as a waterway – have no particular significance. The image of a 'Blue Road', which the Thames evokes for Richard Rogers, is far from their thoughts. Only one thing matters for them: the water in question is a canal cutting their town in two. Like a knife. If they still thought of the canal as having a 'good' side and a 'bad' side, things would no doubt be simpler. But no. What they see when they look out is 'the other side of the canal', a side to which they only venture with reticence, which only deepens the divide and consolidates their set ideas.

In the 19th century, when the canal marked the boundary between city and country, and anyone crossing over in search of business was required to cough up a little ready money as he did so, the canal was king. There was no problem.

At the beginning of the 20th century, however, stubbornness set in, but a harmonious sort of stubbornness. Each side had its own style – older and more business-oriented on the city side, more modern and residential on the suburban side – yet both exhibited a wide variety of splendours. The Boulevard Léopold II, named after the king who created it at the beginning of the 1890s to link the north of the Pentagon with the commune of Koekelberg, was splendid and luxurious. So was the Allée Verte, created at the start of the 18th century on the eastern side of the canal between the Porte du Rivage and the bridge at Laeken. It became a favourite promenade for the Brussels bourgeoisie in fine weather, taking on something of the air of the Champs Elysées. Following the building of the city's first station in 1835, the canal banks gradually filled up with industry and warehouses. But neither was able to impose itself over the other.

This industrial development gradually erased the mundane aspect of this part of the canal, subduing and spoiling it. But two new developments sounded the death knell. The first was in the south-eastern part of the city:

the construction during the 1860s of the Avenue Louise and the creation of the large wood, the Bois de la Cambre, both set to become favourites with the well-to-do. The second, similar but sadder, was the erection in 1957 of a temporary three-lane flyover constructed on pylons along the length of the Boulevard Léopold II. This symbol of progress and modernity, of urban communications and planning, this piece of constructed art was supposed to help visitors get to the Universal Exhibition of 1958, located at Heysel, more easily and quickly. This 'temporary' viaduct remained for almost 30 years, before being exported to Bangkok and ridding the beautiful boulevard of one of the urban aberrations of Belgium's Swinging Sixties.

At the end of the 1980s the problem of the canal started to weigh more heavily. And it was a psychological problem, one of the most difficult to come to terms with. Psychological to the point where the canal's purely economic function was forgotten.

There was no shortage of people, from all sides of the political spectrum, trying to reverse this negative image. And because they were confronted by an artificial construction, every one of them dreamt of turning the canal into a river, a place for leisure. And where was the best place to anchor their dreams? The port zone, of course. For over 15 years this zone gave rise to numerous urban redevelopment schemes.

A Wealth of Redevelopment Ideas

Thus it was that a communal councillor came to suggest the creation of a marina for pleasure boats. This meant cutting a basin perpendicular to the canal, towards the Place Sainte-Catherine, right where in times gone by the basins of the city's historic port had been located.

A little later, a regional Secretary of State dreamt up the idea of creating a sort of

'Brussels Silicon Valley' on the quaysides that would be achieved by creating a green environment and setting up business parks to attract hi-tech companies. At the beginning of the 1990s, the President of the newly created Brussels Capital Region favoured the idea of a residential area, also built around a marina. But this project was far more ambitious than just a leisure port, because it involved a genuine waterside residential district. A canal network was to be excavated alongside the newly constructed Espace Nord business district, looking towards the World Trade Center towers. Along the canal network would be built prestigious residential dwellings. But this project, too, was put on the back burner.

In the end – with the exception of the district located just down from the Place Sainctelette, which was destined for an administrative function – the town planning schemes produced by the Brussels Capital Region favoured an industrial vocation for those sections of the canal located between the Chaussée de Ninove and the Boulevard Léopold II. The central section, on the other hand, was to see a number of initiatives for rehabilitating housing stock.

Alongside the Porte de Flandre, the public played its part in breathing new life into the area with the Rive Gauche (Left Bank) project, a gigantic and innovative project designed to heal the wounds caused by the disappearance of former industries and the tunnelling of the metro in the 1970s.

On the right bank, the redevelopment of the Stock Exchange/Saint Géry/Dansaert district is gradually spreading towards the canal as public authorities improve public areas, and private and public investors renovate housing. This is creativity at its purist: a business centre, fashionable shops, trendy restaurants and contemporary art galleries – all with lofts above.

This nibbling away at the industrial zones is bound to pose a challenge for local public

In 1991, the commune of Molenbeek-Saint-Jean approves four specific development plans, of which one deals specifically with the area around the Canal and the Place Sainctelette, alongside the Tour & Taxis site (on right, not on the plan). This is where the administrative functions will be concentrated – the 'Canal Front' amongst others. Other plans are rather more dedicated to housing and local shops, as the commune confronts the possibility that otherwise it could turn into a grey and dirty urban motorway.

URBAN ASPECTS

Made to measure plans

As soon as the demolition of the 1958 Exhibition viaduct that straddled the Boulevard Léopold II was announced, real estate pressure intensified. The Molenbeek-Saint-Jean commune wanted to maintain the emphasis on quality residential town houses and to spare this long-suffering boulevard from becoming a grey inner-city motorway, dirty and deserted by its inhabitants. It set about a vast planning operation at the end of the 1980s. Its only weapon, although a powerful weapon, was the Specific Development Plan (or PPA). This allowed it to define usages (housing, offices, shops etc) and proportions, to impose preferred perspectives (for example for corner buildings), and to classify existing buildings to allow for or to prohibit their demolition and to tolerate transformation work so long as this work restored the building to its original state etc.

At the same time, the communal authorities decided to attach to the PPA newly created principles governing regional planning charges. These compensated for the construction of more offices than planned by stipulating the simultaneous construction in the area of residential housing, public services and urban facilities.

In order to throttle back speculation without discriminating against previous occupants, a complicated system of charges was established to calculate waivers, which included an exemption for the first 1,500 square metres of office space and a tax on all surface areas exceeding three square metres of office space and one square metre of residential space. The ratio increases to 6:1 for a company occupying the space for itself, and 10:1 if an extension to an existing site is requested by an occupying company.

For more than 30 years the Boulevard Léopold II, which links the city centre to the 'Koekelberg' Basilica, would be disfigured by a viaduct of some 10 metres high, installed in 1958 and running along its whole length. After it was dismantled, important work started to be carried out (road planning, car park areas, lighting, street furniture…) returning it to its former glory.

The impact of the Boulevard Léopold II goes far beyond its strict geographical limits, and thus not one but four PPAs were necessary: A and B applied to both sides of the boulevard, C applied to the area around the Place Sainctelette, and D applied to the Avenue du Port. But all four fell within the same general principle that saw administrative functions oriented towards the canal where the industrial or customs clearance activities of Tour & Taxis were in jeopardy, their large empty sites virtually abandoned.

To guarantee the ratification of its wishes, the commune – and in particular its architect and creator of the PPAs – ensured they had the endorsement of the parties directly concerned. It is therefore no great surprise that the KBC Bank & Insurance Company and the French Community (a department of the Belgian Federal State), whose location here was judged economically desirable, associated themselves with the project via their architects who acted as intermediaries. This permanent dialogue no doubt influenced the PPA, which was approved in 1991, so that everyone was happy – the occupants with the size of their buildings, and the commune in terms of its image.

authorities. Average per capita incomes are increasing noticeably. And the newcomers have nothing in common with the original inhabitants of the neighbouring areas. If their influx turns out to be nothing more than a passing fashion, then coming back down to earth will be painful.

A Vital Economic Powerhouse

Within this vast development programme, the Brussels Capital Region has flagged three major challenges for the years to come.

The first, of course, is Tour & Taxis, whose destiny must finally be decided as a matter of urgency; for without this, the whole of the surrounding district will remain in a state of limbo.

The second challenge, just opposite Tour & Taxis, is known as the 'Heliport' due to its past use. In July 2002 the Brussels government, in collaboration with those currently involved in the area, set down its broad aspirations for this zone, a zone which it described as being of regional interest. Fronting onto the canal was to be a real cohabitation of non-polluting productive activities (for example new technologies) on the ground floors with residential accommodation above. To the rear, and between blocks, was to be a minimum of eight hectares of green areas. Special attention was to be paid to dimensions (taking particular account of the towers of the adjoining North District), the improvement of public areas (for example pedestrian access between blocks, a walkway over the canal towards Tour & Taxis), safety in the Allée Verte, and a new vocation for the neighbouring Citroën workshops, a monument to inter-war industrial architecture that is now mooted as a centralised coach-park (a project under consideration).

The third challenge is located a little further down, just before the start of the Flemish region marked by the viaduct on the Brussels Ring motorway. On the right bank will be built the 'North' water treatment plant, completing the facilities started by the 'South' plant already operating in the commune of Forest. And opposite, on the left bank where a treatment plant for dredged silt is to be located, the thoroughfare alongside the canal will be pushed back to free up space for business parks with direct access to the waterway.

So, eventually the idea of the canal gained the upper hand over the notion of the river: utility reigned over leisure, economics over fancy. And it has to be said that this waterway is a real economic powerhouse for the Brussels Capital Region. In 2002 it handled 6,950 million tonnes of merchandise, 3,752 destined to stay and 3,197 in transit. This was an increase of 7% over 2001 and a record since the canal became part of the Region and the Port of Brussels was created as a regional administration to handle the segment of the canal falling within Brussels.

This increase is in large part due to the restarting of traffic to and from the Hainaut steel industry and the Brussels Capital Region's increased importation of petroleum products. To this can be added the road and rail traffic generated by the port zone, which is an important transit centre for all sorts of products, from construction materials to fruit and vegetables. This increased turnover will be further strengthened by the progressive increase in capacity of the multi-modal container transfer centre that was inaugurated in June 2001.

Too Much Objectivity

The degree to which the desire to preserve economic strength overpowered the imagination is quite astonishing. Not one politician or local or regional authority

attempted – at least with any conviction – to support the natural development of the port zone by introducing a public work of art: a Guggenheim like Bilbao, an Opera House à la Sydney, or even a London-style Millennium Dome – something to attract, at the very least, the curiosity of local inhabitants.

When it became clear that the Brussels Capital Region wouldn't take the initiative, the Molenbeek-Saint-Jean commune demonstrated that it would, despite being one of the poorest communes in the Region. Whilst keeping within its means and territorial limitations, and without deviating from its demands in terms of quality, it set about creating a new façade, a new commercial image on the edge of the Pentagon.

Once the commune started moving, other players appeared: land owners, developers and architects. The first of these, and amongst the biggest, were those who were already familiar with the area.

Entreprises Louis de Waele, which had been located on the left bank of the canal since their foundation, was interested in the moorings on the Boulevard Léopold II. They started by building Jennifer I and Jennifer II, which framed the Place Sainctelette with their complementary forms. In response to the neighbouring Espace Nord development, with its tendency for the vertical and the glazed, the architects A+U and Michel Jaspers & Partners decided on horizontal forms and mineral materials. Entreprises Louis de Waele followed up this development with the reconstruction, between the two new city gates, of Monument aux Installations Maritimes. Then they built a vast office building – also on the Boulevard and using the same two architects – which became the Espace 27 September, the heart of the French Community of Belgium, a department of the Belgian Federal Government.

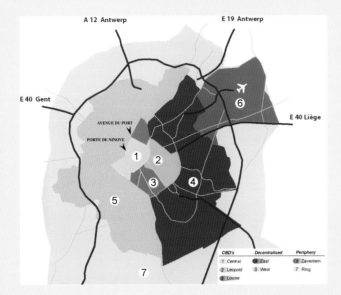

There are seven major business districts in the Brussels Capital Region: the city centre (1a) enclosed within the inner ring road and close to Central Station, extended by the North District (1b), Brussels' mini-Manhattan whose buildings tower over the North Station; the Léopold District (2) – also known as the European District – on either side of the Rue Belliard and the Rue de la Loi, not far from the Léopold District (Luxembourg Station). The Louise District (3) along the avenue of the same name; the 'Decentralised Zone East (4) and West (5), on the edge of the Region, close to Brussels International Airport (6) and the outer Ring motorway (7).

REAL ESTATE ASPECTS

From just a collection of buildings to a real district

Nobody, not even the people of Brussels, foresaw the canal's port zone becoming a business location. For decades the canal was seen as a frontier, a barrier, a rupture. It was first and foremost a legal frontier between the city and the country, with 'right of entry' gateways under which traders acquitted themselves of their transit taxes. It was a social barrier between the commercial bourgeoisie located to the east along the Haussmann-style boulevards and the proletariat living in the Manchester-like swathes of surrounding industrial land. And finally – even today – it is a psychological rupture that separates the disciplined and organised centre from those uncontrolled and unsafe districts lacking any real focal point.

To arouse the interest of developers, to get them for once to venture out of their preferred districts, the canal needed a touch of flair. This took the form of a tunnel passing beneath the water and the Boulevard Léopold II, and the dismantling of the viaduct which had since the 1958 Universal Exhibition (known colloquially by Belgians as 'Expo 58') disfigured the view towards the Basilica.

From that moment on, the boulevard's immediate neighbourhood and the canal saw the benefits of speculative benevolence.

Several badly and insufficiently housed occupants sought improvement within the area. Developers arrived to support their projects and benefitted from the growing number of people who learnt to appreciate the area. Sometimes these developers played on the anxieties of public authorities and on the intrepid nature of the new economy.

Despite progress, even today the area does not yet command the title of 'district'. There is, without doubt, demand, although with the exception of the French Community that requires 20,000 square metres in the area, this demand is unfocused.

The area still suffers from a lack of variety. There is a dearth of shopping facilities, tourist attractions and cultural facilities. And there is a preponderance of low to medium-quality housing. There is also a lack of public transport – a metro station may be located underneath the Place Sainctelette, but this has yet to be planned. But above all, it suffers from its persistent image as a destitute and insecure industrial zone lacking public facilities. Even the presence of a waterway, which in other places is such a source of added value, counts for nothing here.

To make sense in real estate terms, and to overcome the hurdle of being seen as just a collection of buildings, the port zone needs an anchor, a liaison point. The first is quite clearly Tour & Taxis whose functions are gradually taking shape. The second is a walkway that, via the Boulevard Bolivar, would link this new area to the neighbouring Espace Nord. Some say these should have been present from the start, but as they weren't, they must be completed by the finish.

The KBC Banking & Insurance company, which was already well known in the commune, wanted to relocate its headquarters. It became the second major player. The size, the building schedule, the impact and the importance of the project prompted it to organise an architectural competition, which was considered 'the most obvious way of coming to an objective decision'.

The competition, a rarity in Belgium, was divided into several phases. More than 100 bureaus, from the most discreet to the most visible, submitted entries. Five candidates, each with their own architectural vision, emerged from the first round. Ferre Verbaenen and Bob van Reeth with a daring, original and innovative project. Groep Planning with a carefully considered and planned urban project. ARC with an immense window onto the city. Samyn & Associates with a human-scaled project designed to prolong the typical constructions along the canal bank. And the winners, Jaspers & Partners, whose project was selected 'because of its urban integration and feasibility characteristics, its functionality, its clarity of internal layout and organisation, its atmosphere, its values drawing on the past and its viability'.

The grandeur of this granite and glass palace was to be extended by several hundred metres thanks to two well-known developers, Eurobalken from the Swedish NCC group, and Betonimmo and Investissements et Promotion from the Belgian companies Besix and CFE. The first of these embarked on its venture with the partial support, through a preliminary agreement, of one of the canal-side occupants, the Henkel company. The second consortium started construction at their own risk, but under the watchful eye of KBC Bank who made no secret of its inclination for expansion.

Both called upon the architects who had won the KBC competition, Jaspers & Partners, for whom this area would become a major shop window, both in terms of size and duration – from 1992 until the present day. A modular plan formed the blueprint for the area, with a spirit of harmony that was never repetitive or uniform. The 'Canal Front' was underway.

Picking Up the Threads of History

The Atelier d'Art Urbain's responsibility for conception confirmed the principles already put to good use elsewhere. It abandoned the 'international style' that spewed out buildings capable of being erected in any continent and inhabited by any peoples – regardless of their social or intellectual suitability – in favour of a personalised architecture designed to fit in with the characteristics of the city in question. The location, with its own specific peculiarities thus became a source of inspiration, not to be copied or recreated identically, but interpreted, restated and integrated.

There were three critical moments within this approach. It started with a search for references in terms of shape, materials and colours. These then had to be put down on paper so that the architectural methods could be defined, the proportions made grander and the details simpler. The third critical moment, and the most definitive, was to stand back from this broad-brush interpretation in order to arrive at an original creation.

It is from this point that came the specific style, the sort of 'Atelier d'Art Urbain touch' so in keeping with their name. Easily recognisable, yet fundamentally right: no great cacophony of rhythms, no mixing up of materials, no lack of direction in colours – just an allegorical vision of the regional and historical environment.

There is, of course, a degree of mimicry – the designers recognise this with no false modesty – but blended with a dose of modernity in terms of customs and usage and construction techniques.

Nostalgia has no place in this approach. The Atelier d'Art Urbain wishes to be neither retrograde nor rooted in the past. Although its inspiration comes from the past, this same past is nevertheless looked upon with a critical eye. And with this specific philosophy in mind: architecture is considered above all a constructive art. In other words, an art based upon the idea that mere construction itself is not the be all and end all: hence, the exaltation of the so-called 'unnecessary' – details and effects, which establish a dialogue between the creator and the user.

An Eclectic Whole

In their quest for typically Belgian references, the architects obviously retained the ideals of eclecticism, individuality and an avoidance of urban uniformity. As in culture, façades are varied. All differ. There is no imposition of material types. Plaster and stone live side by side with brick and coloured marble without any clash. All sorts of styles are to be found together, without any one taking precedence over another. Some fade into others that take on new colours from those which came before... and so it goes on.

Within the context of the Canal Front, this 'Belgian style' was of course paramount. But it was complemented by another factor: water. Belgian aquatic inspiration, real or imaginary, was considered too industrial, however. So the Atelier d'Art Urbain went elsewhere in search of a rather more urban spirit, a spirit which would respond to the wishes of the developers and which would easily graft on to the existing constructions to the rear. They turned to the banks of the Meuse, the Seine, the Rhine, the Elbe, the Thames and the Neva. They turned to the shores of the Mediterranean, even the Atlantic. They mused over Venice. They wandered along the Hudson.

The final result is unique in its genre: a drawing together, a high degree of decoration and a high degree of design.

But above all, the architecture of the Canal Front is Belgian. If an eclectic spirit reigns,

To facilitate access to the Universal Exhibition of 1958, a roadway viaduct would be built along the whole of the Boulevard Léopold II, straddling crossroads and the canal and some 10 metres high. Although originally designed to be only temporary, it would remain in place until the middle of the 1980s. Its dismantling and especially the subsequent embellishment works carried out on the boulevard would bring life back to the district and constitute the starting point for the 'Canal Front' project.

OCCUPATION

KBC and the canal

The KBC Bank & Insurance company came into being on 3 June 1998 as the result of a merger between the Kredietbank, the CERA bank and ABB Insurances: three companies each boasting a rich past. The Kredietbank, for example, can trace its origins to 1889 when the Volksbank van Leuven was founded in Louvain as a co-operative society. It later became a limited company and then, on 9 February 1935, the Kredietbank voor Handel en Neverheid. In time this Flemish bank became, through mergers, one of the largest financial institutions in the country. The KBC, whose headquarters are still in Antwerp in the famous Torengebouw, and where it still has a number of premises, has been located since 1946 in Molenbeek-Saint-Jean, at 41 Rue de l'Intendant. At the end of the 1980s the company sought new administrative headquarters. Several locations were considered: the Espace Nord, the periphery, even Mechelen where the bank has its computer centre. But the canal, with which the bank shared an almost 50-year history, proved emotionally irresistible.

Many factors favoured the Avenue du Port: a desire to remain in Brussels, a wish to help revitalise a moribund district, the possibility of extending existing buildings, ease of access, the wide room for manoeuvre offered by a 'made to measure' PPA, and a desire to make its mark on the crossroads of two major thoroughfares and on the image of this part of the city. This was a zone with a difference – a barrier, frontier or hinge. The canal was a sort of no man's land – part industrial, part residential – where it was possible to build in a different fashion from the Espace Nord or along a Haussmann-like boulevard, for example. Here the architecture could be more monumental, grander, more symbolic. The project could be prolonged on an urban scale, which is to some degree what came about with the construction of the Canal Front and, more discreetly, with the construction of the compensating residential accommodation to the rear.

Left: The KBC Banking & Insurance company has had a presence in Molenbeek-Saint-Jean since 1946. At the time, one of its 'ancestors', the Kredietbank, occupied a building on the Rue de l'Intendant, perpendicular to the canal. It later expanded into other buildings in the neighbourhood. The decision of the bank to build its Brussels headquarters on the Avenue du Port was a result not only of the length of time it had been present in this area, but also of the possibility of breathing new life into existing buildings via the new building.

Right: Built between 1929 and 1932 in the Art Deco style for the Algemeene Bankvereniging, the 'Torengbouw' or 'Boerentoren' is now headquarters of the KBC Banking & Insurance company, and is also its emblem. Although it is the first skyscraper in Europe, it is nevertheless considerably lower than its American contemporaries. Built by architects Jan Van Hoenacker, Emiel Van Averbeke and Jos Smolderen, it was to be heightened by 10 metres during the transformation works carried out in 1971 by L. Stynen and P. De Meyer.

there also emerges a specific period in Belgian architecture with Art Deco and its rounded forms, its decorative motifs and its numerous details that embellish the construction. Some, including Maurice Culot in his essay entitled *Soyons Art-Deco* (Let's be Art-Deco), don't hesitate to talk of 'neo-Art-Deco' with Brussels being 'The' capital and 'New Brussels' (the canal bank district) its principal centre.

The composition is axial, classical and emanating from 19th-century models which themselves grew out of the Renaissance. The rules of composition and superimposition are observed: foundations and lower levels, projecting cornices, recesses and sloping roofs. The architectural system is not modified. Composition remains logical even if it has aims other than the purely structural: effect, symbolism and imagery. Contrary to the post-modern attitude, which considers that history is an enormous well of shapes from which one can draw willy-nilly and without rule or regulation, the approach of the Atelier d'Art Urbain favours the logic of ancient architecture rather than unfettered originality. Turning this into reality requires recourse to current construction techniques (standardisation and pre-fabrication) together with, as a corollary to this, an artificial dimension of separation: separation between the interior and the exterior, separation between function and expression. The construction system subjugates itself to the image. As for choice of materials, the classic mixture of blue and white stone was the most obvious. The bricks of industrial architecture give way to the majesty of the more noble materials to be found in prestige buildings.

There is, however, a degree of industrialism to be found in the architecture of the Canal Front – the profusion of metals (roofing, window frames, columns, and even whole sections of wall) and glazed areas – but this is achieved without becoming systematic. There is also a 'port' element, particularly in the towers, which are reminiscent of the 1930s and lighthouses or large storm-lamps, in the archway resembling a bridge, and in the frieze representing waves and in the fountains. But the whole complex will also recall for some a Marseilles harbour-master's house or a colonial-cum-seaside administrative building in Casablanca. For others it will recall an Otto Wagner project (such as the Schützenhaus) or certain buildings in St. Petersburg or Hamburg.

And it shouldn't be forgotten that into this Belgium-Industry-Port mixture is introduced the 'Atelier d'Art Urbain touch'. This is seen in the abundance of ornamental details (nail and studding work, bowls, brackets, suspended features) and in the ever-present dislocation of form, with its recesses and promontories which, while they may not shock or surprise, at least serve to attract attention.

From Power to Conviviality

For our erstwhile visitor, who first cast his eye over the original sheds, the length of the constructed canal front appears to be broken up by a more liberal implantation, a pavilion style largely achieved through small squares and gardens located behind fences, and somewhat less through recessing. And complementing this exterior fragmentation are the interior atriums, corridors and mezzanines. This is a far cry from the city centre's Haussmann-inspired boulevards.

When seen from the other side of the canal or further away, it is the monumentality of the buildings that impresses. But above all, housed within the same language and the same vocabulary, it is the multiplicity of expressions, ranging from power to conviviality, from the appealing to the human.

The Canal Front today should not be thought of as an 'urban revolution' or a 'landmark project'. But neither should it be characterised as a 'compromise', although compromise it inevitably is: a compromise between the criteria of public authorities and the indispensable real estate developers, investors and architects. Because what has emerged is not so much a succession of eclectic buildings, constructed side by side as a genuine façade along the canal front, but the fruit of a constant architectural direction and conceptual philosophy. And its great advantage is that whoever designs future projects along the canal – whether they be Altiplan, Archi 2000, Cooparch, Groep Planning, HOK or even the Atelier d'Art Urbain (which has reference points both above the Place Sainctelette and on either side of the Porte de Ninove) – this 'Belgian-style' ensemble will be safe.

RUE AD. LAVALLÉE

BOULEVARD LÉOPOLD II

RUE DE L'INTENDANT

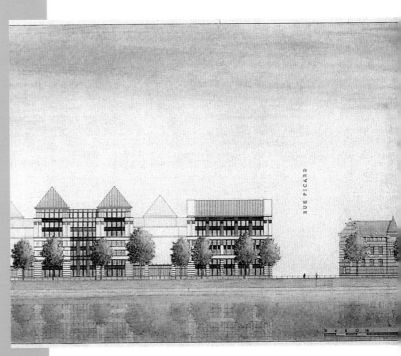

The Projects

KBC Bank
Headquarters

Above: The bank as seen from the canal

Right: The bank as seen from the bridge

KBC Bank Headquarters

Avenue du Port 2
Molenbeek-Saint-Jean
(Brussels)
1992–1994

This was the first building on the new 'Canal Front' and it heralded a new construction phase along the banks of the canal and the Rogier-Koekelberg thoroughfare. The KBC Banking & Insurance company's building is a monument to this new district within the city, a veritable temple of granite and stone.

But is this just another example of new town planning and the new architecture that goes with it? Not necessarily. The two are not obliged to cohabit, especially when you consider that although the KBC was looking for something original, convivial and functional for its head-quarters, it was certainly far from demanding out-and-out avant-gardism. Instead it was looking for a classic institutional image with neither blemish nor questionable taste, a timeless style to aptly represent a banking institution. The building therefore references the archetypal image of a bank, with all the prestige, power and luxury that implies.

Although the headquarters are the extension of an existing building (41 Rue de l'Intendant), this made-to-measure construction builds on a wealth of tradition: noble mineral materials, a two-level pyramid format and recurring classical details and references. Firmly rooted in the Molenbeek soil, this building now forms part of its inhabitants' environment and collective memory. It is an important reference point and represents a major stage in the evolution of the Atelier d'Art Urbain. It is 'over-designed', right down to the last detail, and exudes a certain youthful grandiloquence. It also makes use of current techniques in terms of equipment, conception and work scheduling. The evocation of the past is a mere surface effect, a decorative element, with a traditional tripartite structure of podium, body and roof. The building is exceptionally efficient and functional in every aspect – the interior layout in the offices and common areas, the strong room and service areas, the partitioning, the false floors and ceilings... It also offers excellent communications, with 17 lifts, four of which exclusively serve the underground parking levels. It is equipped with air-conditioning (double VAV system and ventilo-convectors), 875 parking spaces, acoustic insulation, security systems and centralised technical management.

For some people it is 'rational prestige architecture'. For others it is reminiscent of the Brussels 'Palais de Justice'. Though

Above: The retail banking headquarters

Right: The Kredietbank competition – original drawing

separated by more than a century, the same eclectic formulae and attractive and symbolic principles underpin the conception of both buildings. Formalist with reducing parallelism in the eyes of the first group of people, an irreproachable architectural interpretation for the second. For there is undeniably a degree of eclecticism in the accumulation of references, materials and ornamental details. Not to mention the stage setting, the rhetoric, the monumentality.

But this is a special type of monumentality, discernible on two levels. The first is urban: its role as a landmark in the city. The second is more intrinsic: its relationship with humankind, as projected by the entrance hall's impressive framework. The building speaks two languages, for it combines intimate areas (offices, corridors and meeting rooms, which neither surprise nor seek to posture) with spectacular areas (an imposing covered central courtyard, a 500-seat cafeteria, a total above-ground surface area of 38,320 square metres and four basement levels totalling 36,545 square metres): the sprawling format of a town within a town on the one hand, and the calmness of an artificial space on the other.

By opting for a hierarchical, centralised format, the designers were also attempting to fulfill the requirement for 'light for all'. This desire to create a pleasant working environment resulted in the conception of a fanciful system of atriums – a sort of modified version of the ancient agora – and of interior gardens. The aim was to encourage human contact and communication, to bring the exterior nearer to the interior and to provide a maximum amount of natural light. The layout deliberately mimicked the great international

Above: Main entrance arcade

Right: The secure entrance lobby towards the welcome desk

Opposite: Access towards the central atrium

hotels, with a certain exaggeration of meeting areas. This may be considered as a waste of precious space, but the idea that the gross/net ratio is poor is an illusion. Not one square metre is lost. The office-area density is high, and if certain options seem frivolous or unnecessary, upon closer inspection the reasoning behind them is revealed. This is why, for example, the 900-square-metre strong room is, amazingly, located on the third floor. Its security derives from the fact that it is in full view of everybody, and it profits from its location in pleasant surroundings that allow for longer periods of use.

The building can be seen as an extension that culminates in the crescendo of the 10-storey central tower, which casts a nod at the factory tower that once stood on the same site and forms a link with the existing KBC buildings, not to mention those urban accents that distinguish it as a banking institution within the Brussels landscape.

Around the edges of the section formed by the four office towers, between which rise the central atrium and the glass-covered gallery walkways, a series of lower volumes radiate over four levels to ensure continuity with the differing scales of the existing industrial buildings and residential dwellings. The transition from the towers to the existing buildings at the edge of the site is achieved by the clever use of glass that covers the restaurant areas. This axial composition flows naturally from the building's location at the intersection of two important urban thorough-fares: the canal and the Boulevard Léopold II. The principal axis is perpendicular to the canal. It gradually makes its way from the main entrance, symbolised by a great steel archway, towards the large atrium before finishing, via a series of secondary atriums, at the company restaurant, the cafeteria and the old KBC building.

The elevation of the building, despite its pyramidal and stepped composition, fails to completely conceal its size. It dominates. It doesn't submit. The rhythm is constant and the language is directly inspired by classical

compositions, but reduced in number and increased in size. Optical effects are all around: the play on materials, colours, protrusions and recesses. Stone dominates, with red granite and white stone for thickness. To these are added glass and metal (aluminium for the door casings, steel for the entrance construction), tempering the mass of the construction itself. The roofing design in pre-lacquered zinc also helps to diffuse the volumes. An octagonal corner pavilion marks out the local agency, while a metallic ornamental façade feature signifies the main building entrance.

Beneath a lowered arch, the entrance with its cortege of succeeding areas (entranceway, porch, main hall, lifts and sumptuous stairways) is witness to a marvelously orchestrated work of art, worthy of a magnificent theatre set. While the exterior is a profusion of decorative elements (bands, embossed details, St. Andrew's crosses, modillions, studding work, transept arms, cornices and friezes), the interior culminates in a decor that pervades the whole space (tiles, coloured marble and granite wall coverings, alternating natural and artificial light, light fittings designed by the Atelier d'Art Urbain, parallel passageways and metallic walkways linking the towers, intermingling artworks, planted areas, winter gardens with benches, water features and wood-working). The delimitation between the inside and the outside has deliberately been kept slender, although the building does have a certain introversion in its composition. The paradox between transparent and opaque is also intimately linked to the function of this end of the 20th-century palace, symbolising the opposites of public and private, of what is secret and what is common.

Left: The central atrium skylight – detail

Above: A side atrium

Top left: A side atrium water fountain

Top right: A side atrium water fountain – detail

Above left: A major door in the atria – detail

Above right: The restaurant staircase – detail

Opposite above: Typical floor plan

Opposite below: Ground floor plan

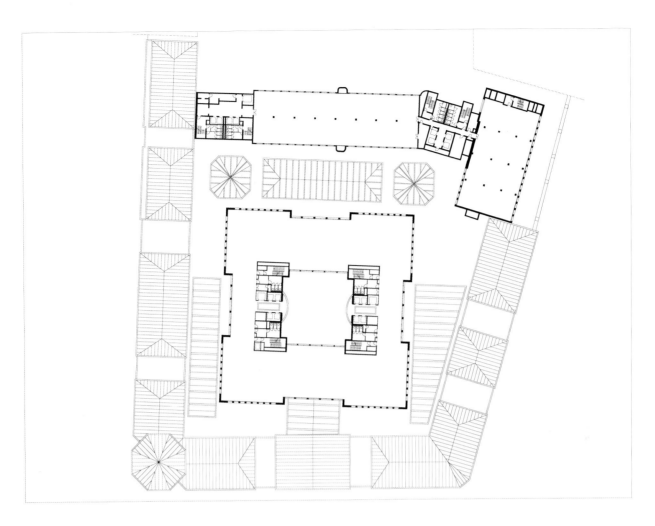

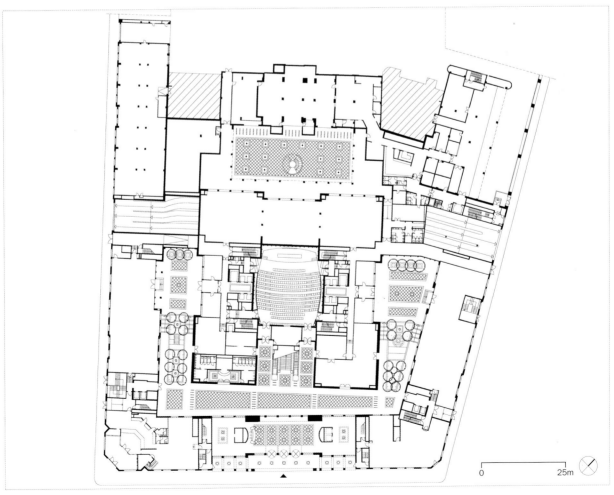

KBC Bank

KBC Bank

Avenue du Port 6–8
Molenbeek-Saint-Jean
(Brussels)
2000–2002

Somewhat strangely, the second building on the 'Canal Front' has never had a name. For a few months it was known as the 'BIP', allowing developers Betonimmo and Investissements & Promotion to launch it on the market. Even before the structure was up, KBC Bank had decided that this building, with its 20,000 square metres, would make a welcome addition to its portfolio. So the building duly lost its three initials but saw nothing arrive to replace them, save for the name of its new occupant, 'KBC Bank'.

Opposite above: KBC Bank Headquarters and KBC Bank global view

Opposite below: Avenue du Port's façade

Below: View from the other side of the canal

The bank's attraction to the building was firstly the result of its neighbours: this acquisition neatly filling the hole between its headquarters and Green Island. But it was also the result of its capacity as an investor. The building was actually conceived of as a development project and benefitted from a number of advantages in terms of flexibility: two autonomous buildings, two entrances, two car park entrances and exits and two sets of technical equipment. If by chance the bank turned out to have been a little over-ambitious, it wouldn't take much refitting to allow one or more tenants to come and join it.

On the canal side, the layout has the look of a reversed 'E'. In reality, it is a double-conjoined 'H'. This configuration was imposed by the need to harmonise carefully with existing structures to the rear, but above all by the need to bring some equilibrium to its neighbours on each side – a 'temple of marble and granite' on one side and a 'green and secure island' on the other. The KBC Bank headquarters chose to place its gardens on the inside, while Green Island chose to put them on public display. So KBC Bank decided to place its gardens on both sides: discreetly at the front behind fences, and more openly at the rear, although sober and inaccessible to its occupants. The first building of the series opted for sober tones, the third for white, so the second would be decorated in cream stone and blue-grey steel. And so it went on, in terms of the general expression and size: the KBC Bank was positioning itself halfway between the large-scale monumentality of the KBC Bank headquarters and the simple, normal-sized discretion of Green Island.

Above left: Offices' main entrance

Above right:: The pergola and the entrance pavilion

Opposite: Main façade – detail

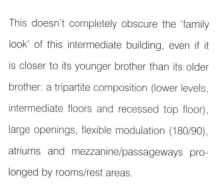

This doesn't completely obscure the 'family look' of this intermediate building, even if it is closer to its younger brother than its older brother: a tripartite composition (lower levels, intermediate floors and recessed top floor), large openings, flexible modulation (180/90), atriums and mezzanine/passageways prolonged by rooms/rest areas.

Because a buyer emerged well before construction was finished, the building was capable of adaptation to his tastes and requirements: the entrance halls were reorganised (only the entrance to number 6 remains as such, both in terms of role and prestige, number 8 received only secondary treatment), the sanitary installations were moved, security was upgraded (bullet-proof windows were installed on the ground floor), a room on the first basement level was reserved for access control and computerised security management, and the quality of the acoustics and ventilation was improved.

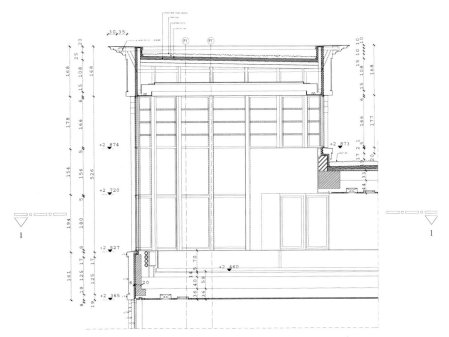

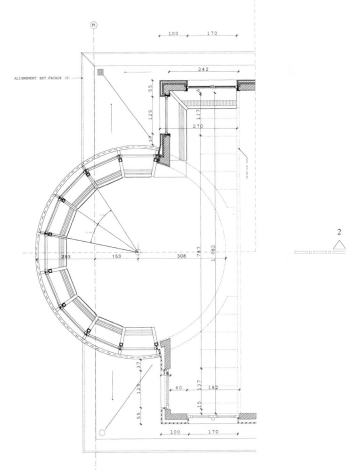

Because KBC was already connected to the developer of Green Island, it requested that the finishings were in the same general style, such as pale coloured marble flooring with elongated encrusted elements in pink and dark green marble, a patinated look to the walls inspired by the Venetian 'patolato' technique and unvarnished and uncoloured beech furnishings etc.

The KBC Bank is a central element on the Canal Front, a liaison point between the KBC Bank Headquarters and Green Island. It is also, perhaps, the Canal Front's most theatrical element and the one that sits most comfortably within the port area in which it finds itself. As an example, you only need look at the three bands in steel or lacquered aluminium that simulate a trio of waves surrounding the building, or even more so at the treatment of the turrets that are the very image of fog-lamps. This 'unsheathing' is even more noticeable at night, when the illumination of the building displays its amplitude to the full.

Opposite above left: A turret and the canal

Opposite above right: A turret – detail

Opposite below: A turret

Above: Penthouse turret – detail plan

Opposite above: Main lobby and access to the elevators
Opposite below: The mezzanine overlooking the main lobby
Below: The elevators – detail

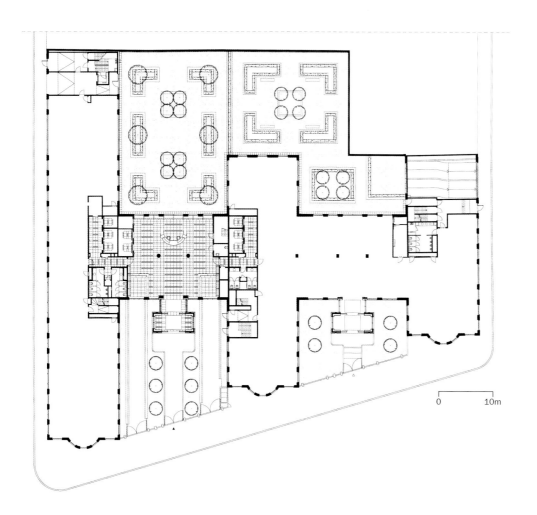

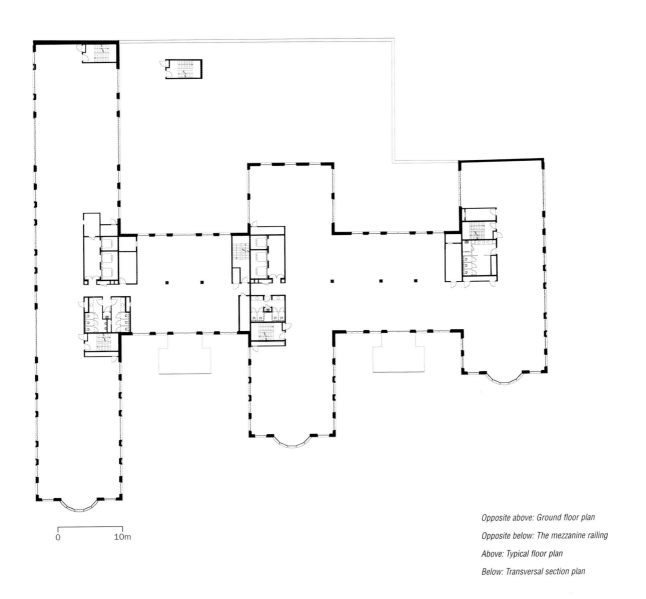

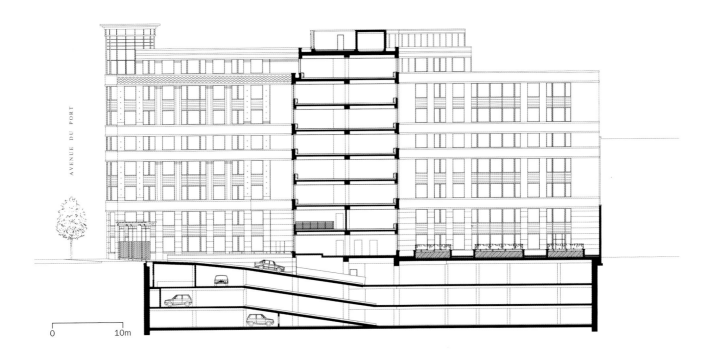

Opposite above: Ground floor plan

Opposite below: The mezzanine railing

Above: Typical floor plan

Below: Transversal section plan

0   10m

A V E N U E   D U   P O R T

0   10m

Green Island

Green Island

Avenue du Port 12–14–16
Molenbeek-Saint-Jean
(Brussels)
1993–1998 (in 2 phases)

The name of the second building constructed along the Canal Front, located at the end of the row alongside the Tour & Taxis warehouses, alludes to its setting. It is introverted, a sort of 'green and safe island within a sombre environment' as its developers Eurobalken style it. These same developers, as chance would have it, had already selected the Atelier d'Art Urbain for this project before the selected firm had even won the KBC competition.

This development project was built in two phases between 1993 and 1998. It was destined for a number of companies, including Henkel who had already been here for a number of years, before the KBC got involved in the act. The project's guiding principles revolved around flexibility, economy (particularly in terms of energy consumption), security, comfort and the cost-effectiveness of the lettable areas.

The philosophy at work here, which was fundamentally different from that adopted for the bank's headquarters building, gradually fell

Opposite: First patio and entrance pavilion

Above: A façade facing the first patio

Below: First patio and its access towards the offices

Opposite above: The Avenue du Port façade

Above: Towards the entrance pavilion in the second patio

Below: Avenue du Port – rendering

into line with the bank's needs, at least in certain areas: the fitting out at the rear of a 2,000-square-metre trading room and modification to the permit, the removal of the two opposite entrance doors (leaving just one), the creation of extra meeting rooms and further modifications to the technical installations, and the materials and interior layout.

Less prestigious, less monumental and less institutional, this complex, which takes in two existing façades on the corner of the Rue Picard and the Rue Bouvier, is nevertheless strong and powerful. It is hinged around two courtyards, its jagged form resembling an 'E' facing the Avenue du Port. This option offers higher efficiency in terms of occupation, and responds to the desire for intimacy, outlook, integration and detachment. It rejects a uniform, compact frontal aspect in favour of a series of sequences, projections and recoils with various different planted areas. This decision to open the complex towards the Avenue du Port required a particular treatment for the lateral gables that directed passers-by to the entrance. The rear, by contrast, presents a uniform façade broken only by a passageway to the Rue Le Lorrain that allows access – during office hours only – to the two courtyards.

Green Island was conceived in a similar manner to the two other projects. Its references and vocabulary are comparable, as are the colours, materials used and its tripartite composition with lower levels, intermediate floor and final floor. It does, however, bring a lighter feel to the whole complex: stone (blue and white) gradually gives way to metal (aluminium and zinc) and glass – the tones becoming lighter the closer the green gets to the blue. The classical proportions of the building, marked at the lower levels, are less pronounced higher up. This vertical escalation is expressed not only by different materials and colours but also by an intense play on relief and ornamentation: studding, inlets, pilasters, sculptured panels, triglyphs and friezes.

The convivial aspect of the courtyard side, with its fountains, planted areas, lighting bowls and benches contrasts with the more prestigious elements of the reception and meeting areas: luxurious entrances, meticulously designed halls and passageways using materials including marble, granite, coloured beech and old-style patinas. The interior areas, consisting of vast flexible floors with technical cores and constructed according to the principles of economy (prefabrication), functionality and efficiency have resulted in technical installations adaptable to the requirements of the occupant, a flexible layout based on a 180-90-180-90 cm modulation that allows for offices of 360 and 270 cm and high-performance insulation for the façades – precise technical and functional features that play a discreet role, hidden from view. Features which impressed not only the Mipim 2000 jury but the Fiabci developers federation, both of them awarding the building with prizes.

Opposite: Entrance grid in the second patio

*Above: Existing façade integrated into
the side façade*

Below: The sidewall and its studs

Opposite: A sidewall – detail

Opposite above: The other lobby

Opposite below left: The welcome desk in the other lobby

Opposite below right: Wooden desk in the other lobby – detail

Above: Mail lobby in the first patio – welcome desk

Below: Access to the elevator lobby

Below: Towards the welcome desk

Opposite above left: Towards the glass gallery

Opposite above right: The mezzanine and its railing

Opposite below: Elevator lobby – red Alicante
marble elements

Housing

Le Jardin des Fonderies

Above: Global view from the common garden

Below: The Fonderies before renovation

Opposite: The garden elevation and its entrance – rendering

Le Jardin des Fonderies

Rue de Ribaucourt
135–137–139–141
Molenbeek-Saint-Jean
(Brussels)
1996–1998

Résidence Van Meyel

Rue Van Meyel 14–22
Molenbeek-Saint-Jean
(Brussels)
2001–2002

Le Lorrain

Rue Bouvier 14 and
Rue Le Lorrain 4
Molenbeek-Saint-Jean
(Brussels)
1995–1997

The Brussels Capital Region's regional planning charges required office-building developers to simultaneously construct residential buildings.

The Molenbeek-Saint-Jean commune was one of the first to put this idea into practice, specifically in relation to the rebuilding of the Canal Front district. There is one medium-sized residential building for each of the three office buildings located within the geographical limits of the Specific Development Plan (or PPA).

Although each of the principal players in the rebuilding of the Canal Front district – KBC Banking & Insurance (KBC Bank Headquarters), Betonimmo and Investissements & Promotions (KBC Bank), and Eurobalken (Green Island) – chose to respect their PPA

obligations in their own way, they each, nevertheless, called upon the same architectural bureau, the Atelier d'Art Urbain.

This common approach is not reflected in the buildings themselves, however. Le Jardin des Fonderies (which is linked to the KBC Bank headquarters), Résidence Van Meyel (linked to KBC Bank) and Le Lorrain (linked to Green Island) are unique responses to the same situation, whether in terms of renovation or construction. They also formulated the projects differently and allocated responsibility for the works accordingly – here working with sub-contractors, there working directly on the project without intermediaries. The architecture and the range of options included are also different and dependent upon the budget, the limits of regulations and programming, the

often limited risk factor, the recourse to tried and tested methods and the inclusion of certain innovative elements.

For Le Jardin des Fonderies, KBC contracted Brussels Regional Development Company (SDRB) to handle its development while bearing the costs itself. This project was undertaken within the old stove-making factory of Nestor Martin, and has been praised on many occasions – in particular by the 1998 Mipim Awards jury (Residential Developments category) and the Philippe Rotthier Foundation for Architecture (European Prize for City Reconstruction 1998, mention) – as an exemplary renovation, both in terms of the retention of the original industrial character of the premises and in the way it integrates life and new inhabitants into the area. Apart from adapting the old structure to its new use and bringing it up to date in terms of fire safety, security, technical equipment, traffic, parking and lighting, the project includes the laying out of a green area and the construction of a new building in the same spirit as the now inhabited factory, including a new façade and stairwells to the rear.

Résidence Van Meyel, a mid-terrace building belonging to the KBC Bank, houses 23 subsidised apartments and is a mixed development by Betonimmo and Investissements & Promotion. Its architecture is basic with no deviations or excess. It blends into the Brussels residential landscape from which it takes its details, colours and materials.

Le Lorrain is a Eurobalken operation undertaken with a view to improving the environmental image of the rear of Green Island. This corner building houses 30 private but inexpensive apartments according to the principles of the SDRB, with whom the developer formed an association by creating Brulobo (Bruxelles Logements Bouvier). The finishing is simple and the architecture more systematic than that normally created by the Atelier d'Art Urbain. This construction was complemented by the renovation of a town house dating from the beginning of the 20th century, located at Rue Bouvier 14, and undertaken in 2001–2002.

Below left: The garden common to the two residences

Above right: Entrance pavilions and towers comprising the vertical circulation

Below right: An entrance pavilion and its 'towered' staircase

*Above: The Résidence Ribaucourt – the terraces and
their powder-coated aluminium railing*

*Opposite above left: The rear terraces overlooking
the garden*

Opposite above right: Railing and studs – detail

Opposite below left: Garden façade – detail

Opposite below right: Entrance pavilion – detail

Above: Fence grid – detail

Below: Link between the renovated façade and the new façade – detail

Opposite above: Typical floor plan

Opposite below: Ground floor plan

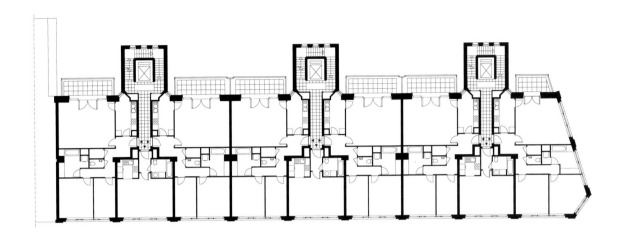

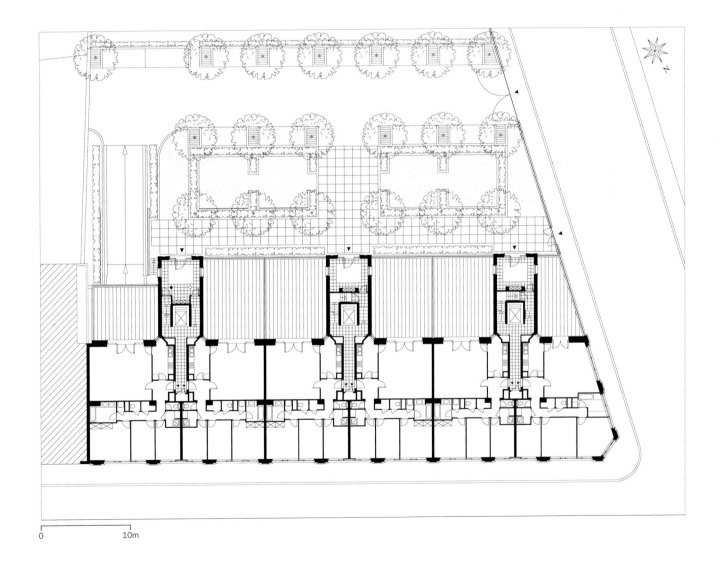

0   10m

Above: The Résidence Ribaucourt and its brick-clad sidewall

Opposite above left: The two residences – global view

Opposite above right: The renovated façade of the new housing

Opposite below left: A typical span of the renovated façade – detail

Le Lorrain

Above: The housing corner façade

Résidence Van Meyel

Below: Transversal section plan

Opposite above: Van Meyel Street façade

Opposite below: Typical floor plan

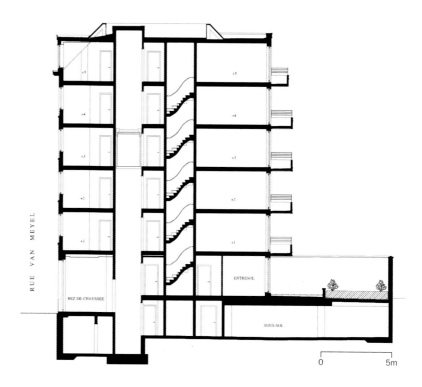

RUE VAN MEYEL

REZ-DE-CHAUSSEE

ENTRESOL

SOUS-SOL

0   5m

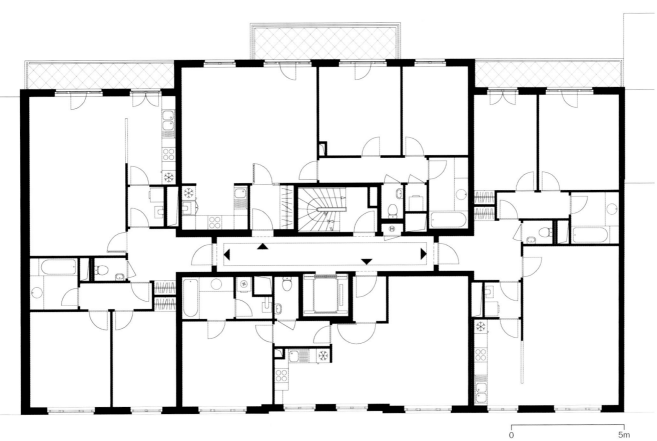

0   5m

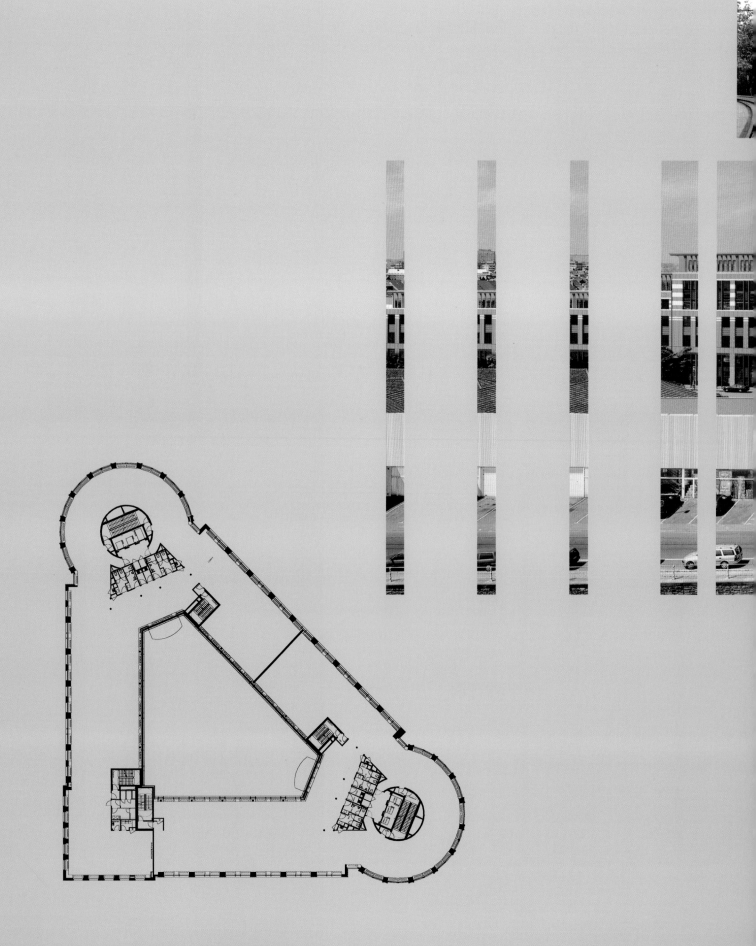

The Projects
Under Progress

Le Lavallée

Bloc Rue Adolphe Lavallée,
Rue Courtois and Rue des
Ateliers
Molenbeek-Saint-Jean
(Brussels)
2002–2005

Porte de Ninove

Place de Ninove, either side
of the Chaussée de Ninove
Molenbeek-Saint-Jean
(Brussels)
2003–2005

Ulens 21–27

Rue Ulens 21–27
Molenbeek-Saint-Jean
(Brussels)
Project

Le Lavallée

*Above: The main façade as seen from the canal –
digital image*

Having already participated in projects located below the Boulevard Léopold II, the Atelier d'Art Urbain turned its attention to the area above it, with two constructions. One is under construction, Le Lavallée, which takes its name from one of the three roads that surround it. The other, Porte de Ninove, is still at the site stage and is located on the square of the same name.

The first project, on the other side of Place Sainctelette, is in the vicinity of the KBC Bank Headquarters, the KBC Bank and Green Island. In a way it seals off Place Sainctelette and prolongs the Canal Front. The second project is several hundred metres away. Running counter to expectations, both projects share the same philosophy, which differs markedly from that of the part-port, part-industrial, Belgian-influenced philosophy that guided the trio of office buildings. Hence there is no symmetry, on either side of the square, not even points of comparison.

This section of the canal, after all, does not disappear into the sea and the wild blue yonder like the other section, but is engulfed by the city. This infinitely more constricted, ordered and urban character meant that the architects had to rethink their ideas. In particular, they had to abandon the scale of the port buildings for a scale more in keeping with the city centre.

With Le Lavallée they decided upon red brick with horizontal bands of white brick above, on white stone (lower levels) and grey thermo-lacquered aluminium and a corner turret, which creates a reference point. In order to keep to the proportions of the surrounding buildings, the three wings of this building gradually slope downwards and the upper levels are recessed. Le Lavallée is set back from the canal behind the row of buildings alongside the boulevard. This meant that the project required an injection of life. This is achieved in three ways: architecturally, by the maximum use of aluminium and glass on the corner; functionally, with the inclusion of shops on the ground floor; and from an urban point of view, by taking up some land to realign the roadway that makes the building an extension of the building on the boulevard that precedes it.

Atelier d'Art Urbain's second creation along the canal and above the Boulevard Léopold II is comprised of two triangular buildings that constitute the new Porte de Ninove, which is on virtually the same spot as the ancient city gate bearing that name and which recognises its function which, like other city gates such as the Porte de Hal, the Porte de Flandre or the Porte du Rivage, was to punctuate the ancient city walls and constitute those points where merchants paid taxes as they passed through. As a way of paying homage to the past and, above all, as a way of indicating the importance of this

crossroads between the roadway (Chaussée de Ninove) and the canal as a point of entry into the city, the architects on this occasion opted for symmetry as a composite element. The lines, however, are more modern, purer and simpler, which illustrates just how far this bureau has evolved and matured, how it has enlarged its range of imagery and set off in new directions.

As well as the Atelier d'Art Urbain's projects in the canal zone, we should also mention those yet to see the light of day behind the Canal Front, like the one yet to be built on the Rue Ulens, for developers Herpain. This will be in the form of an 'L' attached to the KBC Bank, cascading down to the size of the other buildings in the street. A second project, also an L-shaped building, will follow, separated from the first by a walkway.

Left: View of the offices as seen from Boulevard Léopold II – digital image

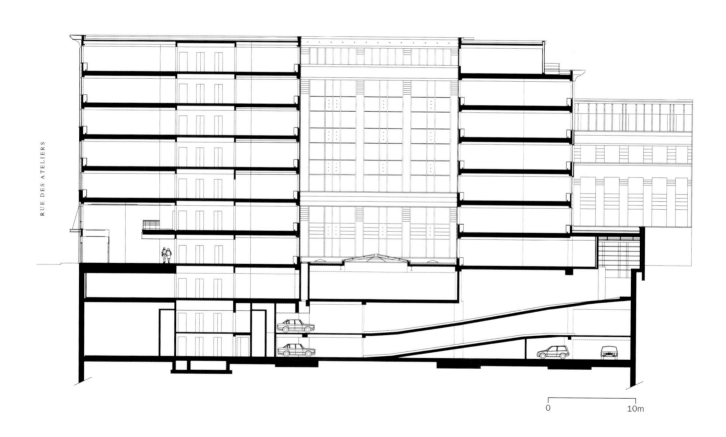

RUE DES ATELIERS

0   10m

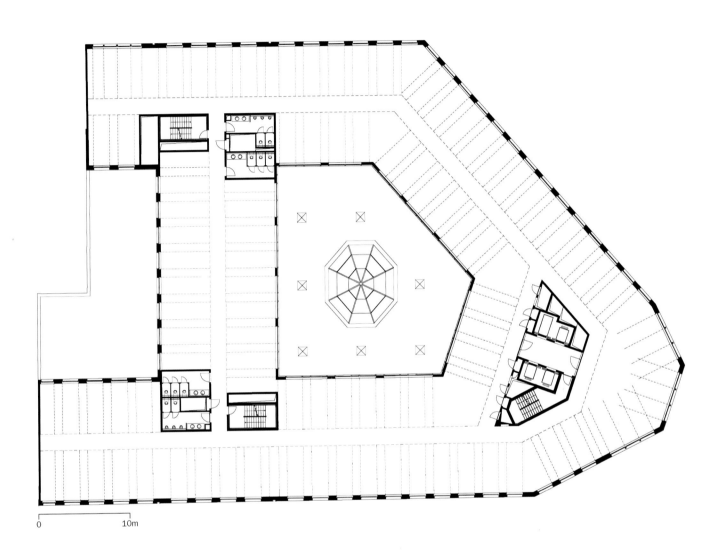

0   10m

Opposite above: Façades facing the canal –
digital image

Opposite below: Transversal section plan

Above: Typical floor plan

Below: Site plan

*Opposite: The future building as seen from the square –
digital image*

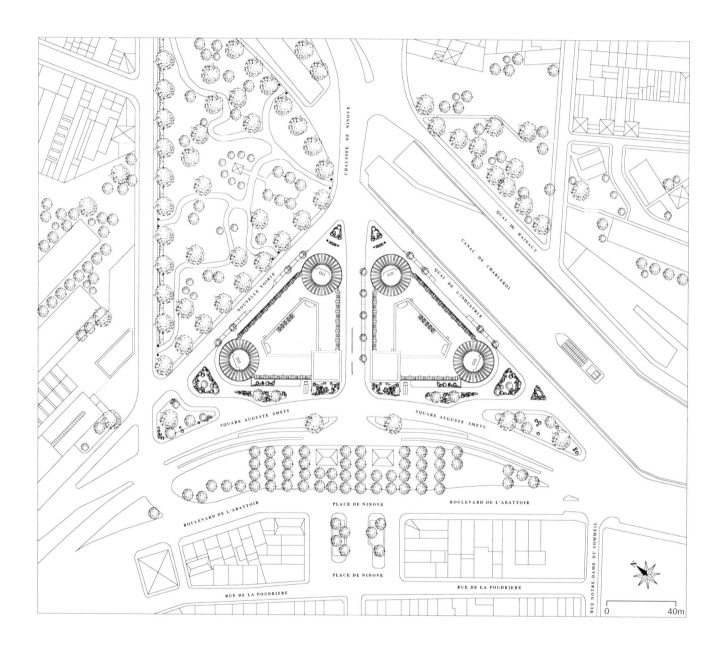

*Above: Global view from the
Charleroi Canal – digital image*

Opposite above: Quai de l'Industrie elevation

*Opposite below: Entrance façade as seen from
the square*

94

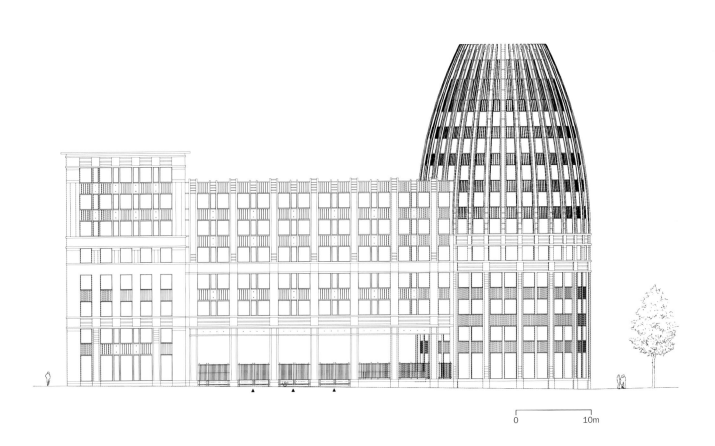

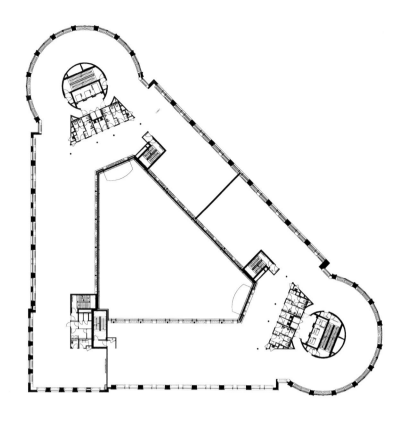

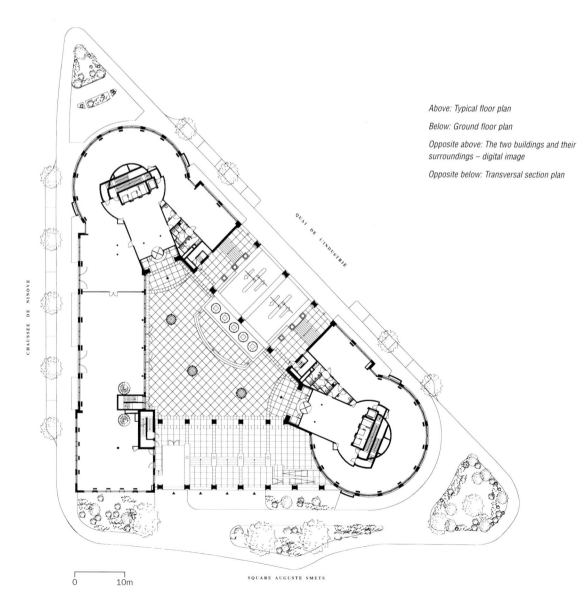

Above: Typical floor plan

Below: Ground floor plan

Opposite above: The two buildings and their surroundings – digital image

Opposite below: Transversal section plan

CHAUSSEE DE NINOVE

QUAI DE L'INDUSTRIE

SQUARE AUGUSTE SMETS

0   10m

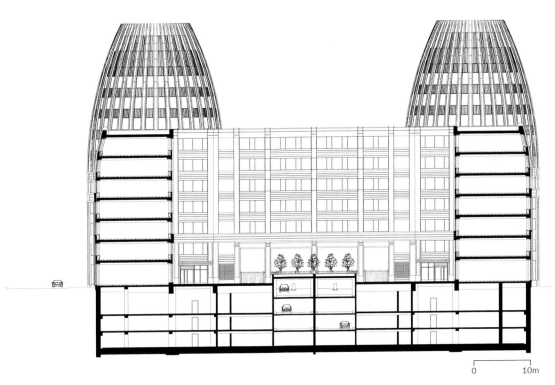

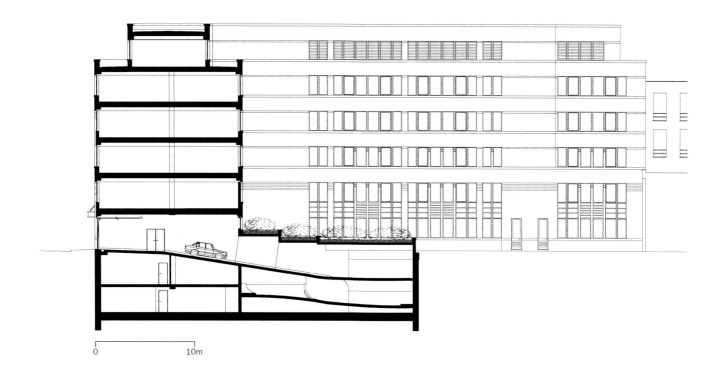

Ulens

Above: Transversal section plan

Opposite above: The KBC Bank – next-door
Rue Ulens façade

Opposite below: Typical floor plan

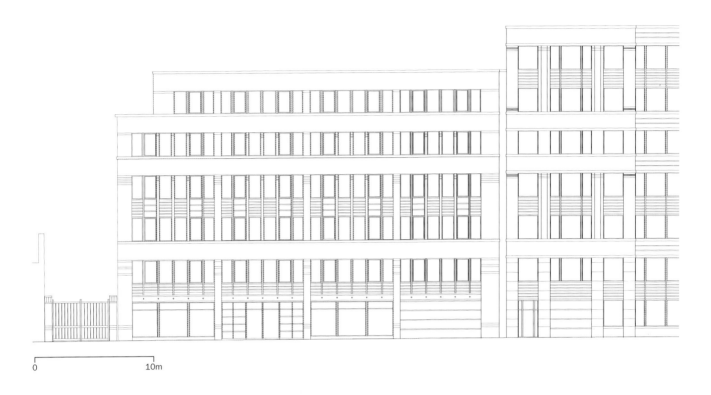

0   10m

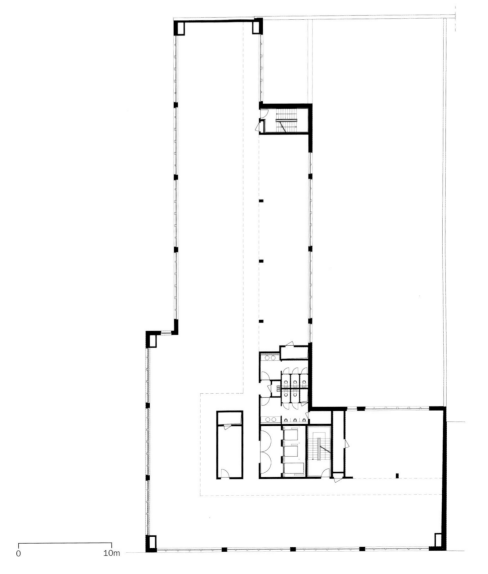

0   10m

Voices from
the Water

Above: Monaco Riviera, Monte-Carlo (Principauté de
Monaco) – hotel, resort, casino, digital image
and photo montage (2006)

Below: Hoboken, New York (USA) – study of the new
marina of New Jersey, rendering (1984)

Opposite above: Riverside Square & Résidence Alphée,
Antwerp (Belgium) – office building and housing
building (1990 & 1997)

Opposite below: Nile City Financial Centre,
Cairo (Egypt) – hotel, restaurant, office and trade
building (2004)

Voices from the Water...

The hotel Klassis on the edge of the Marmara Sea near Istanbul, the Riverside Square and the Arethusa and Alphée residences in Antwerp, The Nile City financial centre in Cairo, the Monaco Riviera in Monte-Carlo, projects in New York and Cleveland, or in Tortola in the heart of the British Virgin Islands.... All in different corners of the world, all with different functions – a school here, a resort there, urban design, office buildings – all these projects are the fruits of the same architectural firm, and they are as diverse in variety as they are in location. The picturesque village, the tourist town, the huge western city, the hybrid megalopolis, the deserted island... A plethora of dimensions and yet with one single dimension in the foreground: water. The calm and peaceful water of an almost forgotten canal, the running waters of a living river, the tranquil, straight yet polluted water of a river transformed into a canal, the flat water of a tranquil sea and the tumultuous, rebellious water of another sea, altogether wilder.

Sometimes bathed in or surrounded by water, such as the project on a Caribbean island or Larvotto Point in Monaco, sometimes located along a waterfront like in New York where a park is placed at the water's edge, all these projects are examples of Atelier d'Art Urbain's use of the most precious of the elements: water. It shapes our cities and our countrysides; it is both a source of life and a symbol. It simultaneously represents leisure, commerce, transport and industry, evoking images of travel and voyages. It is the raw

material of all these projects, be they hewn out of stone or set down on paper.

In contrast with a boulevard, avenue or square, water induces neither a precise typology nor an automatic response. Though it occupies a prime position, this doesn't presuppose a leading role; different interpretations are possible, each case is different. But this by no means suggests that anything at all is permitted, or that only one response is satisfactory. There is an intuitive feeling and respect for the environment that influences and shapes the scenario. Everything depends on how the water influences its location. Is it a link, a limit, a dorsal fin or a final frontier? The attitude to be struck is intimately linked to the site, the programme, the function and the size of the project. Some intrinsic and basic facts accompany these individual manifestations. Water implies a degree of recoil, of distance and of comprehension. These essential factors in the approach to a building induce different options in terms of view, composition and perception.

Left: Battery Park City, New York (USA) – study of the new quarters in front of the WTC, rendering (1984)

The formula of a palace indicating the top of a hill is almost set to music in the case of the culinary college in Tortola, where the villages are traditionally situated at the top of a sea of oil. The option of a symbolic, landmark building moored along a river was put into practice in Cairo with the Nile City. And following the lead of neighbouring constructions, this complex comprising a hotel, offices and a shopping mall rises up to a great height right in the middle of the business district. This type of location further reinforces the presence of water in a city, as is the case in particular within certain districts of London. In the case of the Egyptian capital, the architects accentuated the vertical nature of this complex comprised of three towers set upon a common plinth, while making certain they retained an individuality and a link with the traditions of Levantine architecture: columns, porticos, gilded domes, pergolas, pilasters, mouldings, lateral bands and cornices.

The reference buildings in Brussels or Antwerp aim to return meaning to waterfronts deserted by moribund industry, as was the case with the Docklands in London. In Antwerp, the three buildings Riverside Square and the Arethusa and Alphée residences present a monumental front onto the River Schelde. Their architecture casts a passing nod at industrial, naval and urban constructions, giving an impression of power, which admirably suits both the site and its perception from afar.

The somewhat artistic composition of the Klassis building near Istanbul sees the building set in the hollow of a cliff reshaped by man in order to improve access to the sea. This hotel complex is of Ottoman and local inspiration, and has common features with vernacular architecture recalling villages that grow up naturally around a bay.

In Monaco, by contrast, the objective was to create an atmosphere of water, but in height, on a site completely reclaimed from the sea. Just like the Riviera, the architects conceived a platform of water made up of lagoons set 7 metres above the sea.

So it is that buildings located alongside water can be seen in different ways: from near, from afar, with a slant, in perspective or from a diagonal, but also front-on, from above or from below according to the degree of relief, the degree of recoil and the method of approach. The silhouette – and the multitude of details that define it – of the rooftops, right down to the smallest gap is therefore essential. It is this silhouette that catches the eye, then seizes and keeps the attention.

Above: Klassis Hotel, Istanbul (Turkey) (1989)

Opposite: HLSCC Culinary Arts Centre, Tortola (British Virgin Islands) – culinary school, meeting rooms and restaurants, model (2005)

Historical
Overview

Above left: Battery Park City, New York (USA) – study of the new quarters in front of the WTC, rendering (1984)

Middle left: Klassis Hotel, Istanbul (Turkey) (1989)

Middle right: Radisson SAS Hotel, Brussels (Belgium) (1990)

Below left: Vervloet, Brussels (Belgium) – retail, renovation (1992)

Below right: Consulate of France, Brussels (Belgium) – office building (1993)

Opposite above: Green Water Plaza, Antwerp (Belgium) – office building (1990)

Opposite below: KBC Bank Headquarters, Brussels (Belgium) – office building (1994)

Historical Overview

It is in Brussels, the city where the Atelier d'Art Urbain was founded, where it built up both its strength and its reputation, that a great many of its projects, so typical in style and so instantly recognisable, are to be found. Its influence can also be seen in other places – Europe, Africa and America, for example – encouraging the observer to ask questions. Is this a renovated old building or an old-style new building? Regional in style, or part of an international trend? Simplicity of lines, or an accumulation of over-designed details? Absence of, or quite simply dissimulation of sophisticated technology? The answers to these questions are to be found in the history of this architectural bureau.

A quick look back.

1979

Sefik Birkiye forms an association with Dominique Delbrouck, Christian Sibilde and Grégoire de Jerphanion; all of them, like him, graduates of the Cambre architectural

college. They create the Atelier d'Art Urbain. The title reflects their personal histories, an immersion in the constant urban struggle and the never-ending desire to reconstruct cities. Sefik Birkiye explains:

'During the time of industrialisation everybody preached simplicity, functionality. Everybody was convinced that the needs of man were universal, the same all over the world. Following this period, and in particular thanks to further industrial development, architectural solutions became more varied, more specific. The Atelier d'Art Urbain was born during the period immediately after the cultural crisis of 1968. Like other bureaux, we chose the way of specificity, of an architecture intimately bound into the traditions of a country, a city or a district, but an architecture to which we still wished to give a certain presence, a stature, a soul. What was important wasn't finding an answer, but finding an answer which suited society. Our key word is "humanism". Quite simply, urban development on a human scale.'

1980

This is the time of designs, of perspectives, of getting projects down on paper.

And the time of subcontracting for French architects Robert & Reischen. A step which allows the newly formed Atelier d'Art Urbain to become involved in the demands and the constraints of the profession, and from the very outset to do this by working on large projects.

This constitutes a rich source of learning, and persuades them to repeat the experience over

the following 10 years for other architectural bureaux, including some of the best known: Ausia (France), Teich (Germany), Cooper & Associates (USA), Ehrenkrantz & Eckstut (USA) and Michel Jaspers & Partners (Belgium).

1981

In association with the French bureau Ausia, the Atelier d'Art Urbain wins the architectural competition organised for the ALMA-GARE project in Roubaix-Lille (France), a competition which is very dear to their hearts because it involves social housing and its criteria demonstrate the extent to which society demands an environment which is both high quality and convivial – space with spirit. The

winners propose a solution that represents a return to basics and increased harmony.

1982

Another year, another competition. But this time the Atelier d'Art Urbain wins it on its own: the construction of a 300-room hotel on the banks of the Sea of Marmara, some 40 kilometres from Istanbul, Turkey. With its wide roof areas, its loggias, balconies and pergolas, in vivid colours brought out by decorative tiling, the architecture of the KLASSIS HOTEL (1984–1989) respects local

history, the environment and heritage and at the same time responds to the desires and needs of its users. This win demonstrates that it is possible to construct in harmony with the ongoing historical situation and in harmony with the memories of people and places while still being innovative and contemporary.

1987

At the request of architects Michel Jaspers & Partners, the Atelier d'Art Urbain designs the RADISSON SAS HOTEL (1987–1990) in Brussels and the GREEN WATER PLAZA (1987–1990) office complex in Antwerp. For the former, they bring together modernism and local tradition, particularly through a sort of monumentalising of architectural elements that emanate from the great boulevards and Art Deco. The latter project upsets modernist and neo-classical convictions through its classical and cosmopolitan language. These projects arouse public enthusiasm (exciting local authorities, users, neighbours, passers-by...) and show that a new style has been born: contemporary but caring for the past, inventive, reliant on detail, attentive to the environment, and with roots that are more regional than international.

Opposite above: Villa Palladine, Brussels (Belgium) – housing (1994)

Opposite middle left: Loi 62, Brussels (Belgium) – office building, renovation (1997)

Opposite middle right: Green Island, Brussels (Belgium) – office building (1998)

Opposite below: Le Jardin des Fonderies, Brussels (Belgium) – housing, renovation (1998)

Above left: Le Prieuré, Brussels (Belgium) – housing (1998)

Above right: Novotel Brussels Centre – Tour Noire, Brussels (Belgium) – hotel (1999)

Below: Zurich Assurances, Brussels (Belgium) – office building, renovation (1998)

1989

With Michel Jaspers & Partners, the Atelier d'Art Urbain wins the competition organised by KREDIETBANK (1991–1995) (later KBC Banking & Insurance) for the construction of its headquarters in Brussels alongside the canal; an area too long neglected. The objective is all the more ambitious for this: to create something spectacular, monumental, to give rise to a genuine new constructed waterfront.

1992

The design of workshops and shops for ironmongers VERVLOET (1991–1992) in the buildings of an old Brussels printing works marks not only a new sector for the Atelier d'Art Urbain – industrial and commercial – but also a new approach, for this is a renovation project: an interesting test that enables the Atelier d'Art Urbain to prove that it is not only in newly built projects that modernity and local tradition can be brought together.

1993

When it puts its name to the FRENCH CONSULATE (1990–1993), along with Michel Jaspers & Partners, the Atelier d'Art Urbain pushes the doors of monumentalism wide open. The building is vast with a strong impression of power: a curved façade with a visible pedestal, a pronounced entrance whose porchway and columns rise up on several levels.

1994

The evocatively named VILLA PALLADINE (1993–1994), an apartment building housing 10 luxury apartments located at the edge of Brussels' green periphery, is just one example of the many projects designed by the Atelier d'Art Urbain. In place of the graduated volumes demanded by the local commune's urban authorities, the architects substitute softer, rounded and outward-reaching sections. And to lighten the whole complex and temper any appearance of severity, without denying its character as a solid and grand residence, the roof gardens are fitted out with pergolas.

113

1997

How do you put a tried and tested architectural approach to work in the context of a philosophy for a city? With the renovation of the Brussels office building LOI 62 (1996–1997) and the conversion of the former Nestor Martin factory (also in Brussels) to apartments known as the JARDIN DES FONDERIES (1996–1998) the Atelier d'Art Urbain is able to show that architecture has a major role to play in the revitalisation, even the re-launching of a district. This is equally true of a business district (the Léopold District, also known as the European district) and of a popular district (part of the commune of Molenbeek-Saint-Jean, squeezed between the canal and a boulevard).

It is noteworthy that the success of the Jardin des Fonderies is recognised on a real estate platform as well as an urban planning platform, as it receives a Mipim award in the year of its inauguration (1998) and a mention in the European Prize for urban reconstruction.

1998

Monumentalism has become an everyday concept for the Atelier d'Art Urbain. Though it doesn't stop them from operating on a far more modest scale when circumstances dictate. In Forest, one of the 19 communes making up the Brussels Capital Region, the RESIDENCE DE L'ABBAYE (1995–1998) and two other residential projects which accompany it, the RESIDENCE DU CLOITRE and the RESIDENCE DE L'ERMITAGE, respectively finished in 2000 and 2002, amply demonstrate this capacity to change scales. In these cases it is necessary to take account of the neighbouring town hall and ancient abbey, as well as of the unbalanced architecture of the age-old road bordering the sites.

The Atelier d'Art Urbain has never undertaken private housing, but this is not a barrier to designing. In Brussels, LE PRIEURE (1997–1998) is a large construction full of character comprising four apartments and an indoor swimming pool. This project reflects its setting, charming and prestigious, and is in the spirit of a neighbouring Flemish renaissance style building. This is what leads to the play on brick (natural, and blue and white tinted) and to the juxtaposition of blue stone, wooden window frames and lacquered steel parapets.

With the ZURICH ASSURANCES building (1996–1998) the bureau shows for a second time just how much it has left its mark in the city of Brussels. The previous year it had completely brought up to date Loi 62, a building typical of the 1970s, giving it a totally

new façade, contrasting with the surrounding styles of glass curtain walling. From this comes the majestic ornamental colonnade in red, seemingly imprisoned by white stone. The renovation of the Zurich Assurances building, undertaken in association with the Belgian bureau ELD Partnership, involves grafting a new façade onto the former façade, and a new skin divided into three distinct building sections (two lateral wings treated in white stone, a central section in metal and glass) and into four horizontal strata (a pedestal, a central section, an attic and a final recessed floor).

The Atelier d'Art Urbain takes its conceptual philosophy outside of Belgium once again. Destination: the banks of the Nile, in Cairo, Egypt. They create a large-scale multi-functional project named NILE CITY FINANCIAL CENTRE (1998–2004). The centre is comprised of three towers ranging from 100–142 metres that bring together offices, housing, a hotel and a shopping mall. Its lines recall Levantine architectural traditions, and its spaces demand an arrangement that maximises views towards the horizon and the Pyramids that are within sight.

1999

In 1998 and 1999 the only shopping centre in Brussels city, CITY 2 SHOPPING MALL, receives the Atelier d'Art Urbain treatment. This is a total renovation that stipulates an increase in net space both vertically (through the addition of an extra floor) and horizontally (by taking space in an adjoining building belonging to the same owner). The final objective is to give the project an urban coherence and a degree of continuity within the whole block. The works take in both the residential apartments and the car parks located to the rear. Works also extend to the former Au Bon Marché store to the front, whose ground and first floors return to retail use whilst the upper floors are transformed into offices under the name of CITY CENTER (1998–2003).

For the first time, the Atelier d'Art Urbain abandons contemporary history (with its many examples of Art Deco, neo-classical and eclectic architecture…) to return to the middle ages. At the request of the Accor Hotels group, it becomes involved in the construction of a new three-star, 218-room

Opposite above left: City 2, Brussels (Belgium) – shopping mall (1999)

Opposite above right: Eudip Three, Brussels (Belgium) – office building, renovation (2001)

Opposite middle: Dexia's Management Headquarters, Brussels (Belgium) – office building (2000)

Opposite below: Industrie 10, Brussels (Belgium) – office building, renovation (2001)

Above left: KBC Bank, Brussels (Belgium) – office building (2001)

Above right: Galilée Building, Brussels (Belgium) – office building, renovation (2001)

Above left: Arts-Montoyer, Brussels (Belgium) – office building, renovation (2002)

Above right: Résidence de l'Ermitage, Brussels (Belgium) – housing (2002)

Above middle: City Center, Brussels (Belgium) – office, trade, housing and parking, refurbishment of the Au Bon Marché and new constructions (2003)

Below: Les Grands Prés, Mons (Belgium) – shopping mall, rendering (2003)

Opposite above: Park Avenue, Brussels (Belgium) – office buildings, renovation, digital image (2003)

Opposite below: Nile City Financial Centre, Cairo (Egypt) – hotel, restaurant, office and trade buildings (2004)

hotel: the NOVOTEL BRUSSELS CENTRE – TOUR NOIRE (1997–1999). This is a Brussels military site, a vestige of a defence and look-out system probably established at the beginning of the 13th century: a semi-circular building called the Tour Noire (or Black Tower). In order to ensure that this tower plays a role both as an emblem and as an attraction, the new building encompasses it, but remains detached from it from an architectural point of view: the red-brick façade with white bricks and architectonic concrete casts a passing nod at history in the form of timber-work, cornices, bands and mouldings, as well as a system of loggias across the pergolas.

2000

The second great excursion for the Atelier d'Art Urbain is in Monaco, where it wins an architectural competition for the construction of a new luxury hotel complex (320 rooms and 44 apartments) on the Larvotto Peninsula: the MONACO RIVIERA (2000–2006). Here, again, it is able to demonstrate the bureau's profound respect for local traditions and its distinct propensity for stylistic and structural experimentation. It has to be said that project owners the Société des Bains de Mer, in which the royal family has a majority holding, were also in favour of this: the project's style was to be Mediterranean in spirit, a sort of re-reading of the local historical heritage. This is what the Atelier d'Art Urbain brings to a 10-storey, right-angled building surmounted by three tiled roof areas evoking the traditional architecture of the Côte d'Azur. It includes a tree-lined lagoon fitted with a glazed roundel, a pond crossed by a rustic bridge, as well as several terraces.

The operation to transform the DEXIA MANAGEMENT HEADQUARTERS in Brussels is a perfect illustration of the complementary nature of functional and decorative elements. But for the Atelier d'Art Urbain, this complementary nature goes further. The columns, which conduct the rhythm of the

glass and aluminium façade, are purely decorative. With this building, architecture displays the very essence of its art: decorum. This approach pleases the architects – and will again in the future – so it is brought to the fore.

2001

With EUDIP THREE (1999–2001) located in the European District of Brussels, the bureau goes far beyond the strict limits of architecture and enters the realms of town planning. This project brings together several owners and several buildings, and is a mixture of complete renovation and new building. The objectives are to redesign this complex, which over the course of time has become a mish-mash of buildings and annexes, and, above all, to introduce architectural cohesion in order to arrive at a contemporary solution for this whole block and to return to it some urban harmony.

A vast operation is undertaken on the GALILEE BUILDING (1999–2001) for Dexia Bank. Firstly in terms of image, as the building is strategically located on Brussels' inner-ring road. Secondly in terms of architecture – to create modernity through a subtle play on relief, vertical rhythm, texture and on the colours of material used (natural stone, thermo-lacquered aluminium). And thirdly in terms of the work carried out, because this is a total renovation (only the skeleton is retained) which extends to the interior layout, including amongst other features, the creation of a large-scale restaurant and relaxation areas.

Right from the start of the new millennium, the Atelier d'Art Urbain has been involved in a rapidly re-emerging district: the Midi District, the only district in Brussels that has a TGV station within its boundaries. In just the same way as the three buildings on the Canal Front harmonise with the maritime history of the area, the two complexes running alongside the station – ESPACE MIDI (block A) and FONSNY MIDI (block B) SWISS LIFE HEADQUARTERS

BELGIUM – with completion dates of 2005 and 2004 respectively, pay their respects to their railway environment (metallic materials, light granite, glass…) and emphasise a skyline reminiscent of the New York skyscrapers of the 1930s, with spectacular graduated roofs and rounded corner features. The size of these two projects and the variety of styles in evidence are such that the Atelier d'Art Urbain has virtually created a new street. This impact is all the stronger for the use of recessed and recoiled elements within the architecture, an architecture which does not seek to emulate the existing constructed street front.

2003

In Marne-la-Vallée (France) EURODISNEY go beyond the creation of two theme parks to create a whole new town alongside them, to include a genuine economic hub with a complementary retail centre. The first operation undertaken by the Atelier d'Art Urbain in this enormous project is to create CASSIOPEE (2002–2003) for a Belgian developer, a 10,000-square-metre office building destined to be Walt Disney Company's headquarters.

This year also sees the completion of several large-scale projects in Brussels, Belgium, including CITY CENTER (1998–2003) – an office complex created behind the Art Deco façade of the former Au Bon Marché store. The existing façade is not only renovated, but extended and reinterpreted to allow architectural characteristics sympathetic to the environment to emerge: the juxtaposition of stone and steel, bow windows and numerous ornamental details beneath an arched roof that make use of glass and tinted aluminium.

Another large project comes to its conclusion in 2003: the LES GRANDS PRES shopping centre, created in conjunction with Paris-based bureau Isis, and located on the edge of the city of Mons in Belgium, some 50 kilometres from Brussels. This building's metal and glass architecture is in the spirit of the great industrial buildings of the 19th century and recalls the city and the station, for both of which it represents a sort of new extension.

During the 1990s, the European District underwent a huge programme of renovation of buildings originally constructed in the 1960s and 1970s, and the Atelier d'Art Urbain plays its part in this. PARK AVENUE (2002–2003) completes the sequence and somewhat refines it. This is not one, but three buildings dating from the 1970s requiring renovation. The lower part of the façade is treated in

granite and less prone to deterioration. The upper part brings together white stone and aluminium sheeting, all brought to life by a play on grey-coloured columns.

2004

The CLOS DES LIPIZZANS (2002–2004) is a residential development comprising 37 apartments totally in tune with its times. Located at Woluwe-Saint-Lambert in the green periphery of Brussels, it is aimed at a well-to-do clientele. It is characterised by contemporary architecture (light beige and grey-brown brick façades, sloping flat-tile

roofs, numerous balconies in architectonic concrete with wood surrounds…).

The outer limit of Brussels city, of which one part is formed by the canal, was originally punctuated by six city-access gates; each flanked by two permit-granting pavilions. Today, very few vestiges of these remain, but amongst those that do are the pavilions at the PORTE DE NINOVE. Two office buildings designed by the Atelier d'Art Urbain will shortly redefine this city gate. The symbolic location of these buildings, and more especially their position in an environment of high traffic and movement, close to the canal and to a popular district, means that they are obliged to be highly visible and to present contrasting approaches. From these factors emerges the cylindrical, almost spatial-looking silhouette.

This year also sees the completion of several projects abroad. Amongst these are the BUSINESS CENTER GLACIS (2002–2004), a new landmark development in the Central Business District of Luxembourg that includes three office buildings, a high-quality 10-apartment building, retail space and a crèche.

This project is undertaken in conjunction with Luxembourg architect Jean Petit.

In the hotel zone of Disneyland Paris (France) the Atelier d'Art Urbain is putting the finishing touches to the MÖVENPICK DREAM CASTLE HOTEL, a veritable 400-room palace inspired by the great residences of the Paris region.

2005

On the site of Marne-la-Vallée, a few kilometres from Paris, outside Eurodisney's Val d'Europe but within its influence, the Atelier d'Art Urbain finishes the DOMAINE DE MONTEVRAIN, a 96-unit residential complex. This project is not so reminiscent of the Haussmann style of the 1930s. However, it features recesses in harmony with its different levels and rounded shapes, which are the order of the day.

It might be supposed that along with maturity the Atelier d'Art Urbain would lose its appetite for contests and competitions. By winning the competition in respect of a former barracks in Mechelen, Belgium, however, the opposite is shown to be the case. CAMPUS BUSINESS PARK is made up of 10 buildings – of which the

Top: Hotel Godecharle, Brussels (Belgium) – rendering
(2005)

Above left: Swiss Life Headquarters Belgium (Espace Midi,
block B), Brussels (Belgium) – office building, rendering
(2005)

Above right: Espace Midi, block A, Brussels (Belgium) –
office building, rendering (2005)

Middle: Monaco Riviera, Monte-Carlo (Principauté
de Monaco) – hotel, resort, casino, model (2006)

Below: Heron Plaza, Brussels (Belgium) – new construction
and renovation, housing and trade building, hotel, life
centre, parking, digital image (2006)

Opposite: EuroVillage, Brussels (Belgium) – housing,
rendering (2007)

central building is highest – separated from each other by a series of squares and open spaces. One particular feature is that car traffic is only allowed on the periphery of the site, whose monumental entrance statement is underlined by two buildings which act as signposts, one round and the other octagonal.

During these last few years the European, or Léopold District of Brussels has mostly seen the construction or renovation of office buildings. Hence, the construction of a four-star, 149-room HOTEL on the corner of the Rue D'Idalie and the Rue Godecharle, close to the European Parliament, is therefore all the more interesting.

2006

Another important project in the Atelier d'Art Urbain's files is HERON PLAZA, a mixed development located along one of Brussels' fine shopping streets and owned by the British Heron group. This project has the twin aims of bringing a balance back to the living environment, with residential dwellings, shops,

a hotel and services, and of regenerating a faltering commercial district. Contemporary in architectural style, it respects the collective memory of the city, particularly in the way it blends into the spirit of boulevard buildings. The block will be divided into two distinct parts, one commercial and one residential, linked by a new private road.

2007

Just as it is involved in the construction of a new hotel in Brussels' European District, the Atelier d'Art Urbain is also responsible for the design of the associated residential complex: EURO VILLAGE. Although work on the residential complex started at the same time as the hotel (February 2004), this project, which is split into four buildings totalling 280 units, is not planned for completion in 2005, but 2007. Built of stone and brick, the buildings integrate even further into the existing environment thanks to their graduated appearance. As far as features are concerned, the architects have opted for the strong use of terraces in varying forms.

Canal Front Team

The Team of the Atelier d'Art Urbain

Partners
Sefik Birkiye
Dominique Delbrouck
Grégoire de Jerphanion
Christian Sibilde

Associates
Muriel-Laurence Lambot
Jean-François Dumoulin
Jean-Pierre Vassalli
Catherine Verdood
Olivier Callebaut
Michel André
Michel Larose

Architects in charge
Olivier Minguet
Gaëtan Le Clercq
Luigi Bellello
Dirk Bigaré
François Durt
Laurent Hemelaers
Daria Jezierska
Bernard Colin
Marc Barbier
Gabriel Banice
Karel Lindemans

Architects
Rodrigo Montecino
Cem Kirbas
Florence Chaidron
Jean-Jacques Boccard
Hervé Piérart
Murielle Dasnoy
Catherine Paulissen
François Couvreur
Luc Sulon
Diane Busselen
Bulle Leroy
Claudio Iodice
Patrick Kinsoen
Marleen Poelmans
Isabelle de Clerck
Juan Diaz
Haki Yildirim
Anne Trebitsch
Giacomo Ciani
Gérard Colin
Rita Portugal
Geoffroy Lemaigre
Sarah Camu
Benedikte De Baets
Anne Vandenhaute

Annick Adriaensens
Luc Vujasin
Samuel Jager
Ugur Seker
Fabien Delalande
Olivier Hasquin
David Droesbeke
Bénédicte Lampin
Philippe Genon
Christine Van Elewyck
Frédéric Doerflinger
Chloé Grumeau
Cezary Apiecionek
Ariane Lefebure
Muriel Bettonville
Lambert Jannes
Thomas Royal
Galia Patxot
Marc Favresse
Vincent Dupont
Sylvia Cascione
Joke Vander Mijnsbrugge
Guillaume de Ribaucourt
Olivier De Meulemeester
Frédéric Francuck
Michel Hernalsteen
Jonathan Mike Rothé
Véronique Verhulst
Marie Demiddeleer
Beyhan Saglam
Frédéric Chevalier
Bernard Nève
Frédéric Van Hoof
Christelle Reculez
Dao Li-hu
Esther Plantinga

Project Management
Johan Van Mullem
Etienne Marion
Stéphane Bousse

Administration, Legal & Financial
Brigitte Bruyninckx (Head of Finance and Administration)
Philippe Sochnikoff (Coordinator)
Isabelle Courtin (Economist)
Florence Perlberger (Legal Advisor)
Cécile Verougstraete (Legal Advisor)
Martine Somerhausen (Deputy Director)
Annie Cuvelier (Accountant)
Sabine Gaudissart (Management Assistant)
Françoise Desprechins (Management Assistant)
Donatienne Vierset
Inès Vanderhoeven
Monique Moyson
Vanessa Van Belle
Nathalie Garrebeek

Information Technology
Sinan Akay

Development Adviser
Jacques Boton

Communication
Ante Prima Consultants
Luciana Ravanel

Ogilvy PR
Evelyn Gessler

Publication
Buildings & Data
Georges Binder

123

Project Data

KBC Bank Headquarters Avenue du Port 2 B-1080 Brussels, Belgium

Client: Kredietbank (now KBC Bank)
Architect: Michel Jaspers & Atelier d'Art Urbain
Design and execution: Atelier d'Art Urbain
Structural engineer: Constructor-Courtoy
Contractor: Besix-Van Hout

Above ground area: 60,000 square metres
Underground area: 40,000 square metres
Use: Offices
Number of levels: 4 B + GF + 9
Garage: 738 spaces
1992–December 1994

KBC Bank (aka BIP) Avenue du Port 6–8 B-1080 Brussels, Belgium

Client: Betonimmo (Besix Group) –
Investissements & Promotion (CFE Group)
Architect: Atelier d'Art Urbain & Michel Jaspers
Design and execution: Atelier d'Art Urbain
Structural engineer: Atenco
MEP engineer: Air Consult Engineering
Contractor: Van Hout – CFE

Above ground area: 20,500 square metres
Underground area: 12,000 square metres
Use: Offices
Garage: 278 spaces
Number of levels: 3 B + GF + 7 + Tech
1999–December 2001

Green Island Avenue du Port 12–14–16 B-1080 Brussels, Belgium

(Phase 1)
Client: Brustar One (NCC Group)
Architect: Atelier d'Art Urbain & Michel Jaspers
Design and execution: Atelier d'Art Urbain
Structural engineer: TCA
MEP engineer: LEB-axtro – Tractebel Development
Engineering
Contractor: Van Laere

Above ground: 10,672 square metres
Underground area: 5,617 square metres
Number of levels: 2 B + GF + 6
Use: Offices
Garage: 151 spaces
1993–December 1995

Award: Mipim Awards 2000

(Phase 2)
Client: Eurobalken
Architect: Atelier d'Art Urbain & Michel Jaspers
Design and execution: Atelier d'Art Urbain
Structural engineer: TCA
Mechanical engineer: Solitech – Tractebel
Development Engineering
Contractor: Van Laere – Thiran

Above ground: 25,320 square metres
Underground area: 9,700 square metres
Number of levels: 2 B + GF + 7
Use: Offices
Garage: 154 spaces
December 1998

Award: Mipim Awards 2000

Le Jardin des Fonderies Rue de Ribaucourt 137–139–141 B-1080 Brussels, Belgium

Client: SDRB-Société de Développement de la
Région de Bruxelles-Capitale
Architect: Atelier d'Art Urbain
Structural engineer: Bagon
Mechanical engineer: Bagon
Contractor: Socatra
Above ground: 4,220 square metres

Underground area: 1,150 square metres
Number of levels: 1 B + GF + 5
Use: Housing
Garage: 24 spaces
Exterior parking lot: 11 spaces
1996–January 1998

Award: Mipim Awards 1998

Résidence Ribaucourt Rue de Ribaucourt 135 B-1080 Brussels, Belgium

Client: SDRB–Société de Développement de la
Région de Bruxelles-Capitale
Architect: Atelier d'Art Urbain
Structural engineer: Bagon
Mechanical engineer: Bagon
Contractor: EGTA Contractors

Above ground: 1,320 square metres
Underground area: 220 square metres
Number of levels: 1 B + GF + 4
Use: Housing
1995–October 1997

Résidence Van Meyel
Rue Van Meyel 14–22 B-1080 Brussels, Belgium

Client: Van Meyel (Betonimmo – Investissements & Promotion)
Architect: Atelier d'Art Urbain
Structural engineer: Ellyps
MEP engineer: Concept Control
Contractor: Illegems – M&M Bouw

Above ground area: 2,250 square metres
Underground area: 650 square metres
Number of levels: 1 B + GF + 4
Use: Housing
Garage: 17 spaces
August 2001–March 2003

Le Lorrain
Rue Bouvier 14 and Rue Le Lorrain 4 B-1080 Brussels, Belgium

Client: Eurobalken
Architect: Atelier d'Art Urbain
Structural engineer: TCA
MEP engineer: LEB-axro – Tractebel Development Engineering
Contractor: Socatra

Above ground area: 3,650 square metres
Underground area: 1,065 square metres
Number of levels: 1 B + GF + 4
Use: Housing
Garage: 21 spaces
1996–December 1997

Le Lavallée
Rue Adolphe Lavallée, Rue Courtois and Rue des Ateliers

B-1080 Brussels, Belgium

Client: Immomills-Louis De Waele – Allfin
Architect: Atelier d'Art Urbain
Structural engineer: Ingénieurs Associés
MEP engineer: Tractebel Development Engineering
Contractor: Louis De Waele

Above ground area: 40,000 square metres
Underground area: 20,000 square metres
Number of levels: 1 B + GF + 6
Use: Offices
Garage: 138 spaces
February 2003–January 2005

Porte de Ninove
Quai de l'Industrie, Chaussée de Ninove and Square Auguste Smets

B-1080 Brussels, Belgium

Client: Watan
Architect: Atelier d'Art Urbain
Structural engineer: Solid
MEP engineer: Solitech
Contractor: Besix

Above ground area: 19,781 square metres
Underground area: 9,755 square metres
Number of levels: 3 B + GF + 10
Use: Offices
Garage: 198 spaces
April 2004–June 2005

Ulens
Rue Ulens 21–25–27 B-1080 Brussels, Belgium

Client: Herpain
Architect: Atelier d'Art Urbain
Structural engineer: Studium
MEP engineer: Coget
Contractor: Herpain

Above ground area: 5,995 square metres
Underground area: 2,920 square metres
Number of levels: 2 B + GF + 6
Use: Offices
Garage: 31 spaces
April 2004–June 2005

List of Credits

Photographs

Airprint
41

Atelier d'Art Urbain
72   below

André Baranyi
22   above right

Bastin & Evrard sprl
63
111   above

Jean Boucher
112   above

Serge Brison
33
108   below
110   middle right, below right

Fabien de Cugnac & Associés sc
24   below
26   below
40   above left

Marc Detiffe – MD sprl
Jacket front
26–27   above, middle
28   above
30   above
32
36–37
37
40–41
42–43
46   above right, below
54–55
56
57   above
61
62   below
68–69
100–101
103   below
108–109
111   below
113   above right
114   above left, above right, middle
124   KBC Bank Headquarters
    Green Island

Yvan Glavie – Photo Graphy
14
28   below
34
35
38
42

44–45
46   above left
48–49
50
51
52
54
58
59
62   above
64
65
66
67
70
71
72
74–75
75
76
77
78
80
81
82
83
107
112   middle left, below
113
114   below
115
116   above left, above right,
    above middle
124   KBC Bank
    Le Jardin des Fonderies
    Résidence Ribancourt
p 125   Résidence Van Meyel
    Le Lorrain
Jacket back

courtesy KBC Historical Archives
p 22   below left, below right

Celine Lambiotte
8
122

Marcel Loli
120   below

**Malvaux/Sergysels; courtesy Les
Entreprises Louis De Waele**
16
18   below

Mehmet Mutaf – Viz Tanimitim ltd Sirketi
106–107
110   middle left
117   below

courtesy Schüco
57   below
112   middle right

Sherif Sonbol
100   above
103   above

Luc Wauman
110   below left

Renderings

Atelier d'Art Urbain
24–25   middle
25   above
30–31
58–59
70–71
73
100   below
102   below
108   above
110   above
118   middle
119   below

Commune of Molenbeek-Saint-Jean
18   above

Michel Dugeny
119   middle

Patrick Van Der Stricht
116   middle
118   above
119   above
120   above, middle left, below
121   below

Digital Renderings

Atelier d'Art Urbain
84–85
86–87
90
120–121   middle

courtesy Catella Codemer
20

Détrois s.a.
24   above
85
88–89
93
94
97
102   above
117   above
118   below
125   Le Lavallée
    Porte de Ninove

Model Makers

Ama sprl
120   below

Archetype sprl & Yvan Gilbert
24   below
26   below
40   above

Gedif
120   below

Index